REMNANTS & REFLECTIONS
... from a half-century
in the writing trade

Chris Wohlwend

Cover art by Charlie Daniel
Back cover photo by Jim Bennett
Design by Bill Davison

216 Sarvis Drive · Knoxville, TN 37920

Copyright 2024 by Chris Wohlwend

To the memory of Frosty the cat
and his favorite Wohlwend,
my brother Ben.

All rights reserved. No part of this book may be reproduced or
transmitted in any form or by any means without permission in
writing from the publisher.

Contents

Introduction 1

Wandering 7

Goofs, Gambits & Other Mischiefs 83

At Speed 125

Wandering Again, 2010 151

Opinions Informed & Otherwise 191

Characters & Contention 207

Scuffling.................................... 225

Wordplay 243

Unrealized Concepts 253

Introduction

At a social gathering in 2016, a friend introduced me to two female acquaintances with the description "he's been all over the world."

So, at their request, I named a few places where I had spent time: Australia, Chilè, Jerusalem, Cairo, the Caribbean, Moscow, Soviet Central Asia, and, the place I save for last when describing my nomadic tendencies, Irkutsk. Then they asked if I had been in the military or involved in other government work. At my negative response, they pressed for a further explanation for my wandering. I finally said, "curiosity."

Later, it occurred to me that "curiosity" could explain why I had worked in journalism since I was a teen-ager, starting parttime at Knoxville's morning daily newspaper in 1965 as I started my sophomore year of college — as a marketing major. And, when I was confronted with the question 50 years later, was still working in journalism, free-lancing travel stories.

Along the way, I met James Noel Smith, a fellow East Tennessean, when we were teamed up at *The Dallas Times Herald* in the early 1980s. A quick-sketch master, he provided many of this book's images, including the frazzled and bearded me that accompanies this introduction.

I had started my newspaper career as a copy-boy running errands, soon progressed to writing obituaries and three-paragraph shorts about car wrecks involving fatalities. Then came the copy desk, editing and writing headlines, followed by longer stories, both news and features, covering sports, deciding how stories would be "played", directing other writers in stories to pursue, working with illustrators and photographers and designers in putting together pages and sections.

The various positions led to various cities. After leaving Knoxville to wander around Europe, I returned home and landed a job at *The Miami Herald*. Then there were positions at *The Charlotte Observer, The Louisville Times, The Dallas Times Herald, The Kansas City Star, The Atlanta Journal-Constitution*. A couple of monthly city magazines broke up the daily grind, in Dallas and Atlanta.

Because several of those publications were partners in syndicates, my work ended up being published around the country, and, in one case, in Europe's premier English-language daily, *The International Herald-Tribune*, based in Paris.

Along the way, I realized that my curiosity about the why's

and how's of particular events was a key element in my wanting those stories told and published. And I realized that underlying many of those stories was what I saw as intrinsic truths: life is often colored by absurdity, that my career had been influenced by wonder at mankind's foibles.

My interests naturally led to an attraction to like-minded work cohorts, writers and editors and photographers who shared my beliefs. Newsrooms were full of such thinkers, so as an assigning editor I had no problem in finding writers who looked at news events and their makers the same way I did.

Perhaps the best examples of my ferreting out such personalities happened in Dallas and Kansas City.

At the *Times Herald,* I had noticed a two-paragraph item about the central-Texas town of Crystal City erecting a statue of Popeye, the comic-strip character who got his strength from spinach. With Popeye's help, Crystal City was declaring itself the Spinach Capital of the World. So I walked over to co-worker Susan Stewart and answered her questioning look with the word "spinach." What about it? she asked.

"Crystal City is erecting a statue of Popeye," I said.

After we shared a chuckle, she started making preparations for a trip to Crystal City to report on the thinking behind a small farming center spending money on a human-size likeness of a cartoon character.

A couple of years later, when I was editor of *The Kansas City Star's* Sunday magazine, a young man was charged with murdering an older woman who had befriended him. His reason? He wanted her new orange Corvette, a difficult motive to conceal. He was stopped and arrested while driving her car. The day the story broke, one of my staff writers hurried to my desk. "Did you see this?" Jim Kindall asked, waving a copy of the morning edition. I nodded — and he began working on the narrative of the tragedy. The result won national accolades.

In 1994, when I moved back to Knoxville, I reconnected with a friend from high school. As we caught up, she remarked on my travels, and my moves from city to city, from job to job. "You've certainly led an interesting life," she pointed out as she continued to question me about particular positions. Finally, she said, "You should write a book." I confessed that I was planning one. This is the result.

My traveling went beyond changing jobs and cities. My initial European wandering began in August 1972 when I landed in Luxembourg, the starting point for a journey that lasted until my money ran out — a couple of months. I went back in 1973 on vacation from *The Miami Herald*. In 1977, I spent 22 days in the Soviet Union, Moscow to Georgia to Central Asia to Siberia. In 1978, I was back in Europe for a couple of weeks. Then there were travel-writing trips to Chilé, Australia, Barbados and Israel. An eleven-week European trip built around teaching a four-week class in Cyprus followed in 2010. Details of those trips are included in the two **Wandering** sections.

Just as some of my career moves were difficult to explain, many of my story ideas begged extended explanation before my bosses would allow them. Often, my argument ended with my asking them to "trust me."

Often, selling an idea to an editor proved impossible. But many of those ideas ended up in print later, in other formats or other publications. **Goofs, Gambits & Other Mischiefs** includes several such stories: odd encounters, jokes turned into stoop-sitting tales, work written under a pseudonym, fanciful stories built on factual foundations, and a series of Christmas holiday tales.

An early interest in fast cars led me to races, culminating in a journey to France for the 1979 version of the 24 Heures du Mans, when one of the drivers was actor Paul Newman. That section is called **At Speed.**

Though my ideas didn't always meet with easy acceptance I was lucky to work for like-minded editors in a couple of places. In Louisville, it was Greg Johnson, whose policy was: "It's always better to tell [chief editor's name here] we won't do it again than it is to ask permission beforehand and be turned down." In Dallas, Kerry Slagle adroitly finessed the high sheriffs of the *Times Herald,* insuring that our endeavors made it into print.

Opinions Informed & Otherwise includes a handful of pieces built on unusual approaches to pop culture.

Talented writers often presented problems of a different sort, mostly having to do with story length and deadlines. And, occasionally, battles over use of a particular description, or in one case, the elimination of a comma. Three of the more memorable reporter/writers are described here in the **Characters & Contention** section.

The next section features accounts of jobs undertaken after I walked away from my final full-time newspaper job

— *The Atlanta Journal-Constitution* — in the early 1990s. It's called **Scuffling.**

On a few occasions I was forced to hold story ideas for later pursuit. After I had retired from full-time work, I re-visited some of those ideas, especially those that were fictional. Embracing my East Tennessee background, I came up with the idea of Hillbilly Haiku, perfect for the Twitter format. That led to other attempts at poetry, collected in the **Wordplay** section.

Other notions — most of them absurd on their face — are sketched out under the heading **Unrealized Concepts,** many outdated by the speed of today's computer technology, others abandoned after reappraisal during morning-after sobriety.

Here, then, is the memoir of a writer/editor whose career began in the 1960s' era of typewriters and library trips and continues with today's computers and the Internet, the constants being curiosity and love of the written word.

James Noel Smith's take on the Texas cowboy quick draw

WANDERING

Travels, beginning late summer 1972, encompassing Europe from Norway to Vienna to Spain's Costa del Sol, then a 1977 crossing of the Soviet Union followed by trips to Mexico, Chilé, Australia, and Israel. Featuring terrorism at Munich's Olympics; the KGB and tennis in Tbilisi, Georgia; the Czar's Revenge in Central Asia; Pinochet's fascism in Chilé; camel riding in Australia; and Israel at war.

Europe 1972

In August of 1972, I set out from the familiar hills of my native East Tennessee on what I saw as the ultimate road trip — Europe. I had taken my savings, about $1200, bought an airline ticket to New York and a EurailPass, sold the only decent piece of furniture I owned (a king-size bed), and turned my car over to my dad.

My European destination was Luxembourg — the cheapest flight at the time was New York to Luxembourg offered by Loftleider, the Icelandic airline. A female friend in Manhattan offered to put me up for a couple of days before I left. And I knew that Brussels, my first extended stop, was a quick rail trip from Luxembourg. My European stay — around two months — did not disappoint. Though it began with trepidation, by my second day I was accepting whatever I experienced as part of a great adventure.

Morning in Austria's Tyrol

My first morning abroad, in Brussels, I was jolted awake by loud voices from the street below my hotel room. A peek through the curtains revealed a young couple in a shouting match. The language was French and the upshot was the boy's tearing a suitcase from the girl's hand, spilling its contents onto the sidewalk. She fled in tears, he followed in full shout mode.

As the hoteliers scampered to salvage the suitcase's contents, I prepared for an appointment. In an hour or so I was due at the United Press International office, a short subway ride away. I was to meet Al Webb, another graduate of *The Knoxville Journal's* informal journalism school. Webb was several years my senior and I only knew of him through stories told in the newsroom, many by Pat Fields, a *Journal* co-worker and my landlady. She had written him a note warning of my arrival.

UPI had recently moved its European headquarters from London to Brussels to be closer to the newly minted Common Market, predecessor to today's European Union. Al Webb was chief of the operation.

As I left the hotel the proprietors were divvying up the suitcase's contents, the wife of the pair particularly proud of an electric iron, travel model. I headed to the Grand Place a few blocks away where I would catch the subway.

I found the UPI office without difficulty — it was on the eighth floor of a new building in an aggregation of recent construction a couple of miles away from the stately and historic section that surrounded the Grand Place.

Webb welcomed me and introduced me to the half dozen or so staffers who were present, a couple of them about my age. Both Peter Starr and Mitch Vinocur were from the New York area. There was a photographer from Cincinnati and a couple of Brits.

I was invited to have lunch with the group, a handful of long-haired, scruffy Americans (including Webb) augmented by the slightly more presentable Brits. They would introduce me to cultural differences — the first being "gratuity is included in restaurant tabs, but the restroom attendant expects a tip." The Brits would add an occasional 'bloody Continentals' comment. And everyone agreed that the food in Belgium was much better than what London had to offer.

I agreed to join them after their workday ended, at the King George, an English-style pub popular with transplanted Brits and journalists assigned to the Common Market. It was only a few blocks from the Grand Place, close enough so I was sure I could find it.

As I neared my hotel, I saw the couple I had seen fighting earlier — they were now holding hands. I stopped them and in a halting conversation, told them that the hotel proprietors had confiscated their suitcase and its contents. Then I hurried on ahead so my landlords wouldn't connect me with the lovebirds. Back in my room, I heard the young couple and the hoteliers downstairs.

Curious about the chocolate shops that seemed to be on every corner, I decided to head out for a sample. The scene downstairs? The landlords were helping the couple put their suitcase back together.

A couple of hours later, I was maneuvering through the standing-room-only crowd at the King George looking for my new friends. They introduced me to the excellent Belgian beer — Jupiter and Stella Artois were on tap — and to a Brussels girl named Lieva, the UPI office manager and general helpmate since the move from London. She would be the reason I later ended up on Spain's Costa del Sol.

After three or four days — in which chocolate became a necessary component of every meal and I discovered the devilish Duvel brew with its 8.5 percent alcohol content — I decided to move on to London. There, I reasoned, the natives spoke the same language as I did.

As the ferry crossed the English channel I soon found myself marveling at the White Cliffs, being questioned by customs, and witness to more vents of disgust about "bloody Continentals" from Brits who favor queuing instead of pushing and shoving.

Next, there was arrival at London's Victoria Station. It was early afternoon, Saturday, August 15, and I had noticed a poster for Ronnie Scott's, the famous live-music club in Soho. Jazz bassist Charles Mingus was appearing with his quintet and tonight was the final performance of a 14-day gig. I decided this was a chance I did not want to miss, so I grabbed the first cheap lodging I found, a couple of blocks from the station.

I stowed my baggage in a decrepit room that is noteworthy for having the most inconvenient bathroom of any of my travels: instead of a short walk down the hall, at this place going to the loo involved a trip outside, around the corner and into another building.

Accommodation set, it was back to Victoria Station for the Tube ride to Soho. Ronnie Scott's was easily located and, it being early, the door was open. I walked in and someone — for all I knew it was Ronnie himself — was sweeping. He looked up and calmly answered my panicky question: "Is there a ticket left for tonight's show?" I was assured that there would not be a problem. He asked me if I was from New York, then confessed that he had never heard of Knoxville. I told him I had seen the poster when I arrived from Brussels and hurried over.

He smiled and told me to come back a little before 10 p.m., when the music would start. I thanked him and started to leave, but then realized the poster would make a great souvenir. "You got any posters left?" I asked. Sure, he said, and brought me a mint, rolled-up one-sheet.

So, at about 9:45, I was back in Soho and my newfound friend was seating me immediately in front of the stage and taking my order for a beer.

Soon, I was listening to some incredible music, no more than 10 feet from Mingus himself. Years later, reviewing my notes, I discovered that two of the accompanists, both youngsters, would later become stars. The saxophonist who played with such intensity was Charles McPherson, and Jon Faddis, still in his teens, was on trumpet. At show's end, Mingus, despite his prickly reputation, graciously signed my one-sheet. Framed, it has graced my wall since.

Still high on my stroke of luck, I exited the club — and discovered that Tube service had ceased for the day. Fortunately, London's streets are clearly marked and I found my way to Piccadilly Circus. There a bobby told me how to get back to Victoria Station, a 30-minute walk away.

When I wandered out the following morning I found that the other seven flats that made up the building I occupied carried condemnation notices on their doors, which explained the low rate I was paying. But my room was OK and I didn't mind going outside and around the corner to visit the bathroom.

This time, I set out toward the Thames, in the opposite direction from my route the day before. I soon found myself in front of the Tate Gallery, an art museum that was new to me. But it was open and there was no entry charge. It was the first genuine visual-art museum I had explored. Inside I found dozens of realistic images of regal-looking horses and other livestock, soothingly bucolic. An occasional "riding to the hounds" actioner provided the only change.

Then, venturing into another room, I was introduced to the grandiose canvases of J.M.W. Turner. Nothing soothing about his tributes to English adventure and warfare. After I realized that I needed to put distance between my eyes and Turner's vision, I could appreciate his scale, which of course was appropriate for his subjects. Weeks later I would wonder at the size of Rubens' nudes and other canvases in other museums. Listening in on a museum guide's tour in Vienna, I learned another reason for the scale of the paintings — they were commissioned for huge ballrooms in huge castles.

Soon sated with culture, I left the Tate and found a pub. Now, I could test my UPI friends' low opinions of English culinary options, at least those that I could afford. The pub was called somebody's Arms — but I can't remember whose. There, I had my first pub lunch, a meat pie that I eventually made palatable with a hefty dose of Colman's mustard. From then my London meals were primarily fish and chips or Wimpy's hamburgers. My pub fare I limited to beer, ale, and Strongman's cider.

At the Arms the next day I was joined at the bar by Reg, who introduced himself with an offer to buy me 'alf a Watney's. He had just finished a rough morning, he said. His work? He was a mortician. He and a cohort had picked up three bodies before lunch, all from the homes of the deceased, and each requiring a maneuver down flights of stairs with the stiff.

"Sounds like an interesting job," I said as I bought the next round. "Always something different, mate," he answered. Asked if dealing with dead bodies bothered him, he quickly laughed. "The stiffs don't bother me but sometimes the relatives or the neighbors can get up my nose. One of the blokes today was an old bachelor lived by himself. So the neighbors wanted to know all about him.

"Was he odd? the lady next door asked. She was sure we could tell by the body whether her neighbor was a poofter."

Reg and I shared another laugh or two before he took his leave. "Back to it, mate," he said. "The dead are calling."

I headed across the road to Victoria Station, checked the map for the Tube and decided on the British Museum, Hyde Park, and the other city-center tourist spots. Massive assemblies of bones, the Magna Carta, then outside to acres of well-groomed green, with swans a-swimming alongside.

Heading back to my room, I ducked into a music store to check out the popular records. There, I discovered that prominent display space was given over to American blues and country — Conway Twitty shoulder to shoulder with Willie Dixon.

Early the next morning I found Billingsgate, London's storied fish market. There, I quickly discovered that a solo American with a camera was allowed no slack in the boisterous Cockney-accented maelstrom. Outside, I watched as the market's porters hurried their wares to circling vehicles, dodging buses and cursing competitors as they balanced boxes of fish atop sturdy hats called bobbins. They are constructed of thick leather, a three-layer addition nailed to the top. To be successful, a porter has to be able to balance his wares on top of his bobbin hands-free.

As I dodged one porter, a large fish slipped to the pavement. No problem — with only slight pause he had it back into his hand and then into the vehicle of his customer.

Later, at a curry take-out spot, I discovered evidence of the cross-cultural blend that reflects the colonial past of imperial England. My samosas were brought to me by a Rasta Jamaican as Ray Charles sang the Beatles' "Eleanor Rigby" on the sound system.

The next day I decided to return to Brussels — I needed to solidify plans with my UPI contacts for meeting in Munich during the Olympics.

So I booked space on a ferry headed for Oostende, a popular beach resort destination for the English and Scandinavians. There I joined local revelers at the annual Slufferbal, a beery festival marking the end of the tourist season. An empty compartment aboard the train to Brussels provided quiet for an ample recovery.

Charles Mingus in Copenhagen

Arrangements made, I headed north again, this time for

Copenhagen, where I again ran into Charles Mingus. As he sat at an outdoor table with friends, members of his sextet played with American ex-pat saxophonist Dexter Gordon at a street corner a few yards away, upright piano pulled out to the sidewalk. Twice in a 10-day period I enjoyed brilliant music in a form that originated in the U.S., an ocean's width away.

Later, wandering through crowded pedestrians-only streets, I noticed a tall, bearded young man wearing a horned Viking helmet. As he handed me a brochure touting the wares of his employer, he spoke in English that sounded suspiciously American. When he realized that I, too, was from the U.S., he confessed that he had dropped out of college and then left his Minnesota home to escape the draft.

"Coming to Copenhagen," he told me, "was the smartest thing I've ever done — a great time and beautiful girls. Sure, I have to wear this goofy helmet, but it's still worth it."

The next day at the train station, I watched a delivery of barrels of Carlsberg beer. The means surprised me — the wooden barrels were on a wagon drawn by a pair of huge dray horses. And the horse-and-wagon was not for the nostalgic effect; I later saw other working wagons making such deliveries.

I realized that parts of Europe were still recovering from the effects of World War II. There were coal-fired steam engines at work in rail yards in Luxembourg, in Cologne, in Metz. Along Spain's Costa de Sol, donkey carts were utilized at construction sites where four-and-five-story buildings were going up with trimmed logs being used in place of the two-by-fours found in the U.S.

After my single night in Denmark, it was on to Oslo, for genuine Viking descendants. First evening I encountered two young couples, drunk and looking for an argument. When they realized that I was an American, they started in on "your dangerous President Nixon." When they finally realized I agreed, they invited me into a bar for a beer. Declining, I thanked them and ducked into my hotel — I could have stayed in Knoxville if I wanted alcohol-fueled political discussion.

After studying a map the next morning, I decided to go over the Scandia mountain range to Bergen, on the Atlantic, then take a boat to Flam, the beginning of a famously torturous up-the-mountain rail line to the tiny hamlet of Myrdahl. From there, I could catch the train back to Oslo, then south to Hamburg and beyond.

Saturday afternoon in Bergen's main square: a pristine 1958 Chevrolet convertible, white with red interior, was the star as teen occupants circled the plaza, with frequent stops as the male driver allowed other friends – females preferred – into the passenger seats. But at dark the "Amazing Oskanis" a Czech high-wire act, took over, grabbing the crowd's attention with their skills. The highlight included a vintage CZ motorbike outfitted for wire riding. Even the Chevy occupants were impressed enough to contribute krona to the hats passed by various Oskanis.

Early the next morning I shivered on the ferry as it headed up Sognefjord. Though it was August, Bergen is at Latitude 60.39, a mere 427 miles south of the Arctic Circle.

Most of the train's occupants on the dizzying train ride up to Myrdahl were locals headed back to Bergen; the rest were tourists who remained in the warm comfort of the rail cars for the return to Flam. Since I was headed to Oslo, I was the sole person on the platform for a couple of hours. I discovered wild bushes covered with a small fruit that looked familiar. I tried one — and then sated my hunger with delicious blueberries.

It was late afternoon when I reached Oslo. Studying maps and train schedules, I decided my next overnight stay would be Hamburg, a stop that is only memorable because I watched Olympic competition live on a half dozen different TVs. Television sets were not as ubiquitous in Europe as they were in the U.S. Stores that sold them locked up at night with a set or two left on and facing the street so that passers-by could stop and watch. The games were garnering small groups in front of closed shops.

Heidelberg would be next — but a couple of hours into Germany, early evening, and I had the compartment to myself. I realized it would be midnight when I arrived in Heidelberg and I could comfortably sleep on the train. An inquiry of the conductor led to my decision to stay where I was — the train's ultimate destination was Vienna at 8 a.m. the next day. With the discovery I realized that I could save on hotel bills by taking overnight trains, thereby stretching my money and my time in Europe.

Toward evening, at the Augsberg stop, I was joined by an older man and his adult son. The son understood enough English to tell me that they were from Zagreb, then part of Yugoslavia, and that he had taken his father to visit another son working in Germany. They were now on their way home. Sergei explained to his father that I was American, and we had a limited conversation. I realized that this trip was of great importance to the father, who kept smiling at me and nodding. This was his first trip outside of Croatia, then under the Communist yoke of Marshal Tito. Obviously, he was pleased to meet an American, even if it was one sporting a scraggly beard and ragged jeans.

Then he opened his much-scuffed suitcase, beaming as he showed me the new shirt that his son in Augsburg had given him. He instructed Sergei to show me the other gifts they were taking back. A large bag contained fluffy towels and dresses for his wife and daughter. Then he pulled up Sergei's pants legs to show me the new boots he was wearing.

At Salzberg my new friends exited to change trains for Zagreb. Through the open window I helped the old man pass the bags to his son, and then shook his hand as he grinned at me before his return to the far side of the Iron Curtain.

Vienna at 8 a.m.: a crowded station, an inexpensive hotel room — half the price I had paid in Scandinavia. Then, great music in a park, at no cost; more huge paintings, this time in the Kunsthistorische Museum (huge paintings deserve display space sporting a name with at least 16 letters), where I discovered the works of Pieter Breughel with their depiction of spirited, everyday peasant life. They were much more interesting than the by-now-familiar religious scenes I had viewed in other museums. I ended the day with an inexpensive and delicious Hungarian goulash followed by Sacher torte and halting conversation with a cute and friendly barmaid.

Innsbruck would be next, then St. Gallen, the Swiss city that was home to my ancestors before their immigration to the United States. From there, Munich and the Olympics.

Innsbruck's Alpine surroundings dwarfed everything in the city — it seemed that each street I looked down ended in a dizzily-high snow-covered peak. Needing a better perspective, I took a funicular up the Nordkette mountain to Hafelekar station, transferring to a cable-car on to the top. After taking in the humbling view, I noticed that most of my fellow passengers had set off on well-worn mountain trails, apparently taking their usual route home. At a souvenir kiosk I was greeted by a large, shaggy dog standing on his hind legs. When I said hello to the pooch, his owner emerged from the back of the shop laughing. He was, she told me, her best employee.

As a settling fog began to obscure the view, I caught the cable car for the descent, the pooch barking a good-bye.

On the train for St. Gallen, I ended up in a compartment with three young Swiss returning from a skiing weekend in Austria. They were still in party mode and we enjoyed a raucous conversation until their limited English became besotted by their intake of beer. At around 10 p.m. they started gathering their gear for departure.

"St. Gallen?" I asked. "Ja," they told me. So, as the train slowed I grabbed my bags and followed them to the platform. And, as they disappeared around a corner, I discovered that I had exited at "St. Gall-Ostend" and the small station was deserted. All I could do was start walking, following in the direction the train was headed. This situation, I realized, could be a test of my determined embrace of whatever adventure my travels presented.

Fortunately, after I had walked about a half-mile, a taxi headed in my direction provided a positive solution. The driver spoke some English and was astute enough to realize that I was in need of a hotel on the low end of the price range.

The next day I wandered around St. Gallen, taking in buildings that date from the 1500s. Shops featured the intricate lace, embroidery and other textiles that brought prosperity to the city, though not to my ancestors, who saw better opportunity in the new world.

On the morning of September 5, 1972, I arrived in Munich after departing St. Gallen an hour or so earlier. I was to meet my UPI friends who were working the Olympic Games, which I had been following with stops in front of shops that sold televisions.

On the edge of the Munich station, I noticed a large crowd clustered around such a store. And I discovered that Palestinian terrorists were holding Israeli athletes hostage at the Olympic Village.

Quickly, I checked everything except my camera bag at the station's baggage-storage facility and caught one of the special buses for the games site. Optimistically, I hoped to talk my way into the Village as a reporter/photographer. But I could get nowhere near the Village, so I wandered around the games, mixing with a crowd that had no idea what was happening nearby. Olympic chief Avery Brundage had made the controversial decision to continue the competition.

I decided to head back downtown, where I could at least find a television to follow the hostage story. There, only a few minutes after getting off the bus, I saw a crowd gathering around a shouting man at an intersection.

A German had accosted a pair of young backpackers,

interspersing English into his invective. Judging from his words and his appearance — buzz-cut, salt-and-pepper hair — he was a World War II veteran. The American couple, in their early 20s, were trying to escape their tormentor, who was telling them how he hated all Americans. His shouting lasted only a couple of minutes — he quickly attracted a pair of Munich policemen. As soon as he saw the cops he ran down the crowded street, the policemen quickly following.

As onlookers apologized to the Americans, I asked them what set off the attack. The German "just walked up and started shouting," the girl said. "I guess he saw the U.S. flag on my backpack and that made us a target." They were headed for the train station when the confrontation came. "We've seen a couple of days of the games," explained her boyfriend, "and after this morning decided this is not a place we want to be right now."

Reaching the same conclusion, I joined them on the walk to the station, where I watched more coverage of the attack before retrieving my baggage. Then I boarded an express train headed to Heidelberg. In the compartment I ducked into, talk was dominated by the terrorist attack, but it was in German so I could only guess at the gist by the sad head-shakes accompanying the conversation.

In Heidelberg, I found a room near the bahnhof and watched the still-unfolding Munich situation with the hotel proprietor on a lobby television. Negotiations had led the terrorists and their hostages to the airport, where a shoot-out had developed.

As we watched, the hotelier kept repeating "formidable" in French. When the attack reached its tragic end, he went back to registering me as a hotel guest, then, still distraught over what we had just watched, apologized for assuming that I was French.

I made it to my room, glad to be away from Munich, but still anxious to find a TV in the morning for the latest developments. After walking around Heidelberg, with sidewalk stops to join those watching Munich news on television, I decided to make arrangements to meet a WAC friend who was stationed in Zweibrucken, near the French border.

Phoning her long-distance involved going to the post office, giving the number to a clerk and then waiting until a connection could be made – a process that took a couple of hours. There was no way to reach my UPI friends even if a phone had been available. Contact would have to wait until we were all back in Brussels.

In Zweibrucken, where my friend's military duties involved a first-strike U.S. air base, the mood was serious and somber. And my only memory of two days in Heidelberg is the hotelier and his distraught "formidable".

After Zweibrucken, it was on to Spain's Costa de Sol, which I had to reach by a certain date to meet my new Brussels acquaintance, Lieva. My WAC friend and I challenged a young official at the bahnhof and he came up with a schedule – involving five different trains – that would get me to Barcelona.

There would be a late-night stop in Lyon where I would laugh with a very drunk Frenchman as he saw off a couple of friends with a rousing version of the "Marseille." And then another restful sleep in an empty compartment until arrival the next day in Catalonia.

Barcelona: A waterfront hotel where a room cost me about 75 cents American – and was overpriced. Then, a few steps away at a hole-in-the-wall seaman's café, a similarly inexpensive seafood stew that was so delicious that, after a bowl at lunch, I went back and had another at dinner, much to the amusement of the staff. My other standout memory of the energetic capital of Catalonia is the work of Antoni Gaudi, whose Sagrado Famalia church got more of my time than any other religious edifice on the trip.

By rail, the trip from Barcelona to Malaga is an overnighter, down the Mediterranean coast then through the Sierra Madre before emerging on the southern coastal plain.

I easily found the kind of compartment that I now preferred with two facing benches, capable of seating and bedding six passengers. When I entered, it was occupied by another American — college age — and a young Spanish couple. My countryman had a guitar and spoke some Spanish. Once the train began to move, we were joined by another passenger, a Moroccan.

The newcomer was happy to discover that the musician and I were American. He could practice the English he had learned working on a U.S. military base in his home country. And practice he did — his language dominated by obscenities learned from GIs.

He had, he told us without prompting, been to Genoa to buy a Vespa, which was now in the baggage car. The Vespa, he said, would "make getting girls easy." He then told us in lurid specifics what he liked to do with girls. (The Spanish couple were interested only in each other and didn't understand English, so they were spared the graphic detail).

The guitarist and I soon tired of the Moroccan and went to the corridor. I stopped on the platform between cars to take pictures. There I met a priest who, it turned out, spent most of the journey between cars, where he could smoke cigars. But you can smoke in the dining car, I pointed out. He smiled: "There, too many people bother me with their problems."

Finally, as dark came, I returned to the compartment. The Moroccan had gone to the dining car, I was told by the guitarist. He started playing and then sang a couple of folk standards — I remember "Tom Dooley" — with the Spanish couple listening and smiling though they didn't understand the lyrics.

The guitarist and I arranged the seats into beds and were stretched out when the Moroccan returned — now even more voluble after a few beers. I was on one bottom bunk, the guitarist above me; the Spanish couple shared the other lower bunk, the Moroccan over them. Soon, I was asleep.

Proud Spanish train crew

It wasn't long before I was awakened by angry shouts from the Moroccan. He charged the Spanish couple with keeping him awake, making too much noise cooing to each other. He made them understand by using his hands to indicate the chattering. The loud diatribe attracted the conductor, who quickly directed the Moroccan outside. His angry words faded as he was led down the corridor. We closed the door and locked it.

Shortly after day-break the train screeched to a halt. Looking out the window, I saw the sign that identified our stop as Chapparal, which featured one small building and one large tree. Then people started getting off the train, led by a group

On the Costa del Sol with Lieva

of Franco's finest, in uniform. They commandeered the only shade, under the tree.

It turned out that one of the diesel engines had broken down and we were stuck until a replacement could be brought in. Before long our former compartment mate joined us, spruced up and smelling heavily of cheap cologne. He was cheerful until we asked him what had happened. Then he began cursing the conductor and Spain in general. He had been relegated to the baggage car for the rest of the journey, joining his prized Vespa.

In the train station at Malaga, I caught a teen as he was

about to start rummaging through my bags on the platform. A nearby policeman, seeing the ruckus, hustled him off, but I stayed with my bags until it was time to board a local. Torromolinas was my destination – it was one of the Costa del Sol's first hamlets to discover there was more money to be made from tourists than from fishing.

I found Lieva at her hotel, much nicer than my lodging had been in Barcelona. Torromolinas was all hustle, with beachfront hotels under construction, aimed at the Brits, Scandinavians and Germans who were providing demand. To Lieva's chagrin, I found that the women from northern Europe quickly turn any stretch of sand into a "topless" beach.

And, alone at a bar my second afternoon, I witnessed an oft-happening vacation experience. One of the teen bartenders had just received a letter from a girl from London who was smitten with him a couple of weeks earlier when she was on holiday. He had shared the letter with a couple of compadres and they were laughing as they worked at translating the English.

Finally they hit a word they could not figure out, and since I was handy, they asked my help. The word was "weep" and, using my fingers to demonstrate tears running down a cheek, I explained that the girl was crying because she had not heard from her new Sun Coast boyfriend. As his friends continued to razz the letter's recipient, I paid for my beer and grabbed my bags. Paris was next, and since my Eurailpass was to expire soon I wanted to get as far north as I could before I would have to start buying train tickets.

Changing trains in Madrid the next day, I realized that the conductor had not noticed that my pass was no longer valid, which meant I was good at least to the border. About 10 p.m. that night I walked through the Hendaye station just inside France. I had an hour while the Spanish train morphed into a French train. By now, I had been rail-bound for about 14 hours, from Malaga on the Mediterranean to Basque country on the Atlantic coast. And I was hungry.

In the otherwise dark street, I spotted an open cafe across from the station. There were only two occupants, the proprietor behind the counter, and his friend, on a barstool opposite. They apparently were engaged in a philosophical discussion. (At that point of my European wandering, I was confident of my abilities to determine the nature of such bar talk, weighing the intensity of the participants and whether their drink choices were wine or the more-potent brandy.)

Answering the proprietor's friendly query, I asked if I could get a sandwich. "Oui," he replied. "And an Orangina," I added. Then I realized that I had only a few francs, probably not enough for a sandwich and a drink. I brought out my money — all coins, including a few Spanish pesetas. He took my francs, the price of the sandwich — a chunk of baguette liberally smeared with saucisson. My offer of the pesetas for the Orangina brought chuckles from the pair. The proprietor closed my fingers over the coins and opened the Orangina and poured it into a glass, setting it down next to my sandwich, like the drink served properly, on a china plate. Then he and his friend resumed their discussion while I enjoyed my unofficial welcome to France with a simple and delicious meal.

The next morning, alone in my compartment, I was awakened from a deep sleep by a gentle shaking. It was the conductor. "Paris, Monsieur, Paris," he said.

I gathered my bags and exited the car. Obviously, since there were few people on the platform, the train had been in Gare d'Austerlitz for a while. But despite the lack of bustle and the overcast skies, a palpable energy welcomed me to Paris. Now wide awake, I entered the station and found a place to sit and figure out my next move.

Soon, I was joined by another young American, who told me he was from Ohio, a student at Kent State. Discovering that I did not yet know where I was going to stay, he volunteered that he had met another American on the train, an older man named Tom who now was a resident of Paris.

"Tom lives in a hotel near here with his girlfriend and said we could probably get a cheap room there, if you want to share." Kent said. Tom then walked over, breakfast — a beer — in hand. Introductions were made and we followed our new guide to the taxi line.

During the ride Tom told me that he was a horseman from California, had abandoned family and hearth a couple of years earlier for Paris. "I go to Spain to work on spaghetti Westerns," he said. "I'm the gypsy wrangler. The Spanish can't ride horses cowboy-style, so gypsies are hired. They only work a few days till they get paid, then they get drunk and I have to round them up for the next shoot.

"They make the movies in Spain because the high desert looks like the American west and it's much cheaper than in Italy. So I'm in Spain for a month or so, collect my pay and come back to Paris until I get called for another movie."

Then he laughed. "I guess I do the same thing the gypsies do, except I stay until the job is finished. Then I come here to hang out with my Swedish girlfriend until the next shoot in Spain."

The taxi pulled up to a small hotel on Boulevard Raspail and we clambered out. Tom told the manager that we were looking for a room, then disappeared up the stairs. Kent and I agreed on a price with the manager, but the room wouldn't be ready for a couple of hours so we left to get lunch and do some exploring. We discovered a cheap cafe, where I successfully convinced Kent that he should not ask for ketchup for his pomme frites.

Back at the hotel, the manager told us that he had only one room available — and it was more expensive than the price quoted earlier. We balked, and the discussion quickly turned ugly. He started attacking Americans for having barbecue grills, for eating TV dinners, for using money stamped with "In God We Trust". The latter, he sneered, was the same motto that was printed on the money of Germany's Kaiser Wilhelm.

"That's why he easily marched through France," Kent retorted as we grabbed our bags and hit the street, the manager angrily shouting at us from the hotel doorway. We found a more reasonable hotelier a couple of blocks away.

After a couple more days exploring Paris, shivering on park benches as the weather turned and becoming anxious about what the expiration of my Eurailpass could do to my finances, I reluctantly decided that I should get back to Luxembourg for the return flight to New York. And, because I had wisely signed up for a Loftleider promotion before leaving the U.S., I knew I had one more adventure upcoming. The promotion involved an overnight stay in Reykjavik, Iceland's capital city.

At the Gare de Nord, I boarded a train for Luxembourg and, miraculously, the conductor did not notice the expiration date on my pass had been smeared enough to make it unreadable. As I lugged my bags into the airport, a fellow passenger headed to New York provided an affront to my recently acquired stance as a sophisticated world-traveler.

The outfit of the tall blonde woman had caught my attention – cowgirl hat and boots set off by a fringed and beaded suede jacket. My first thought: another tourist contributing to the "ugly American" stereotype.

But when she walked into the departure lounge, she immediately began talking to her seat neighbors in heavily accented American English mixed with German. She was headed from her home in Mannheim to visit the location of her favorite television show, "Dallas." And she was in full cowgirl mode to ensure that she fit in.

My Icelandic visit was bookended by two seafood experiences. First, there was a smorgasbord where I had my first (and only) tastes of whale blubber and putrified shark. The shark meat is, according to Viking lore, made better by being buried until it's putrid. The taste was one that I did not want to acquire.

Needing to cleanse my palate with a beer, I found an interesting-looking bar on the waterfront. There, a couple of fishermen tried to involve me in the Cod Wars, a dispute between Iceland and the United Kingdom over which nation had the rights to fish-rich waters between the two. The battle ultimately involved gunboats and led to United Nations rulings that were codified into the now standard 200-mile fishing zone determination. Ultimately, Iceland prevailed, costing the UK thousands of fishing-industry jobs.

But on that particular afternoon, I wasn't interested, so I finished my beer and departed, dreaming of a buttered and baked cod steak to counter the blubber and shark. The next afternoon my Manhattan friend and I found an even better solution at a Midtown joint – an American hamburger accompanied by fries and a quart or so of iced tea.

Europe 1973

Though I was gainfully employed again, the next year I decided to return to Europe for Munich's Octoberfest, to continue my exploration of Paris, to visit my friends at United Press International in Brussels. So I took my two-week vacation from *The Miami Herald* and set out once again for Luxumbourg, this time confident in my seasoned-traveler abilities.

In Brussels, I caught up with my UPI friends and took up Mitch Vinocur's offer of a place on the floor of his tiny apartment for a couple of nights. Space was limited as he had two other guests, a college-age couple from the Boston area.

Shortly after my arrival, the other guests returned, the female of the pair in tears – she had lost her purse, containing cash and passport. Mitch and his co-worker, Peter Starr, calmed her down and then took her to the U.S. Embassy to start work on replacing the passport.

"There would not be a problem," they assured her. But the old hands (primarily bureau chief Al Webb, who had offered his help) were not so optimistic. "It will take weeks," Webb said.

I was heading out to Munich after a couple of days, so my only involvement was as an observer. But I did make sure that I knew where my passport was for the rest of the trip.

A fashion photo shoot in Munich

The girl had to be persuaded to call home – she was afraid of family reaction – but finally she did and was reassured.

The next day, after another trip to the Embassy, she and Peter and her boyfriend returned, optimistic that she would have a new passport within a day or two. I thought that was not realistic, but as Peter and I headed to the UPI offices, he assured me that it would happen, and quickly explained why. "She's a Kennedy," he said. And the next day she picked up her new passport.

A couple of days later, in a small square near my hotel in Munich, I discovered a professional photo shoot, apparently featuring female fashions. There were two models, dressed casually in skirts and form-fitting tops in the earth hues that were popular during that era.

It was a chilly late-September day, and the temperatures insured that the models' lack of foundation garments was evident, producing nipply views that explained why most of the onlookers were male. The accompanying photo captures the scene.

Passers-by watched as the girls followed the photographer's directions, laughingly walking toward him before veering toward the church to his left. After a couple of false starts, he got what he was after and the girls proceeded up to the church door before turning to look at the camera.

Suddenly, the door opened and a priest stepped out. The girls' embarrassed look – and the photographer's quick halt – let everyone know that the reverend's presence was not part of the shoot. The photographer and his girls quickly gathered up their equipment and hurried away, lunch-time entertainment at an end.

Octoberfest, understandably, is a blur of memories, not helped by out-of-focus photographs. I remember being impressed by the huge tents, the huge crowds, the huge mugs of cold beer, the huge roar of the Lowenbrau lion, and the areas set aside for throwing up. And there is a vague memory of sitting in front of one of the oompah bands as its membership shrunk one by one, the unwieldy horns eventually bringing down their players. When I finally wobbled away, the group was down to a single, teetering baritone horn.

Somehow, I managed to make it to the bahnhof the next

morning for the train to Paris. There, I met a lone celebrant who confessed that he did not know what had become of the companions he had arrived with a couple of days earlier. "But I must return to work tonight," he muttered. He and I boarded the train and found an empty compartment.

When he told me he was headed to Ulm a few miles northwest of Munich, I pointed out that we were on a train destined for Heidelberg and that the Ulm train was boarding on the adjacent platform.

"Ah, but I have no ticket. So I will be thrown off at the first stop, which is Ulm," he explained. "This way, I do not have to pay."

As soon as the train left the station, he was asleep. At Ulm, the conductor marched him off the train, and, with a bow and an "Auf Wiedersehen" he departed.

In Paris, I found an inexpensive room and then re-traced my steps from the year before – the Left Bank, the Latin Quarter, Le Dome, the cemetery I had been thrown out of because of my camera. This time, I decided, I should check out Sacre-Coeur, where I joined Parisians as they enjoyed a sunny morning on the steps.

Finally, I settled into another Paris tradition at a café near the Gare de L'est – an aperitif at an outside table. Soon, I was in a conversation with a fellow American. He introduced himself as Hal, and said he was from Chicago, though he had been living in Europe for a dozen years or so.

My inquiry as to how he made his living led to an amused

smile. "I guess you could say that I get by compliments of my old man, though not with his blessing." Then he gave me the details, a story that he obviously enjoyed sharing.

"Dad and I disagreed on my future," he told me. "He wanted me to join the family law firm and I wanted nothing to do with that. So I came to Europe. There were angry letters and phone calls but I refused to return to Chicago. Finally, pressured by my mother, he set up a fund for me. I would get a tidy sum each month, to be deposited in my bank account. But, trying to make things as difficult as he could, he structured it with a list of the countries where he would not set up the account. No Paris bank, of course.

"So then I remembered his talking about Liechtenstein and its secretive banking tradition, and opened an account there. But he was one step ahead of me. It was on the no-go list. Then there was San Marino in Italy – again a no-go. But then I discovered Andorra in the Pyrenees, an easy train ride from Paris. And, with my mother adding pressure in my favor, Dad gave up.

"Mom likes to visit a couple of times a year for shopping. And I take the train to Andorra once a month to pick up cash, then spend the rest of my time here with my girlfriend. It is, mon ami, a good life."

And, I told him, with your smarts and the persistence your solution demonstrates, you, too, would have made an excellent lawyer. To that, we drank a toast.

Soviet Union 1977

In August of 1977, I took vacation from my job at *The Louisville Times* and set out for the Soviet Union, signing up for a 22-day tour. With my crisscrossing of the U.S. and travels around Europe, I considered myself a veteran traveler, but I knew this journey would be different.

And so it proved, from introducing Central Asians to Polaroid instant photography to encounters with the KGB; from dodging gourds thrown by an angry Muslim in Uzbekistan to waving at a binoculared and curious teen girl at the Kirov; from witnessing a chair-throwing brawl at a tennis match in Tbilisi, Georgia, to sheltering from an early snowfall on the shore of Siberia's vast Lake Baikal.

Most of my previous travel forays had been solo or with a friend or two, but for this journey I would have to sign up with a tour group, required of American tourists by the Soviet government. At Dulles International Airport, I met my nine fellow travelers, all veterans of international journeys.

Two were retirees from the State Department and a third had lived in India, working for a U.S. health agency. Helen's State Department background included working with train loads of refugees in north Africa. She was traveling with Marie, a psychologist friend who had brought her Polaroid camera. When she took an instant portrait of the hotel manager in Samarkand, he saw to it that our next meal included fresh grapes, which unfortunately led to several of us coming down with the Czar's Revenge. Dick's experience with the health agency meant that he was an expert on intestinal maladies, knowledge that was of great use.

Our U.S. escort was Lilya, a first-generation American whose parents emigrated from the former Soviet Union immediately after World War II. Russian was her first language. Her familiarity with the Soviet system and Russian-language skill would prove essential. The trip would not have been nearly as enlightening, or as much fun, without her presence.

The flight provided a proper introduction. The food was memorable because of its inedibility. I can still picture a rubbery piece of baked chicken of a notable grayish appearance. I opted to wait until our French refueling stop to eat — even fast food at Orly would be better than what was served up by the indifferent Aeroflot stewardesses.

The plane, a Soviet-built Tupolev, was at capacity, primarily with apparatchiks of the Soviet diplomatic corps and/or their families returning to Moscow. Just across the aisle from me and Lilya were three middle-aged Soviet women, each gripping shopping bags stuffed to the bursting point.

When the seat-belt light went off, the bags were opened and the trio began comparing the contents — wigs. The women spent the first hour of the flight trying on, swapping, and giggling. Lilya explained that wigs like these were unavailable in the Soviet Union. "They probably took orders from friends before they departed on their U.S. visit," she said.

Then, in Russian, Lilya complimented the women on their choices, getting beaming smiles from the be-wigged trio.

As our flight neared Moscow, Lilya told us what to expect with Soviet customs. Printed material would be carefully examined. No Playboy magazines, no books that depicted the USSR in a light that wasn't favorable as defined by the Kremlin apparatchiks. Such publications were in high demand, Lilya told us. I was carrying Desmond Smith's guide to Moscow, and it caused a short delay when the customs officer confused it with Hedrick Smith's book on life in the Soviet Union, which was banned. A supervisor was summoned and after a few minutes of looking and conferring, my guidebook was handed back and we were ushered through.

A quiet moment in Red Square

Just outside the customs area our Intourist escort, Anya, introduced herself. She would prove efficient, a staunch Communist — and a hidebound apparatchik. By the next day, Lilya, Helen, Marie and I were working on ways to circumnavigate Anya.

The bus ride into Moscow introduced us to Soviet architecture and suburban planning — complexes of multi-story, gray-concrete buildings surrounded by unkempt fields crossed by worn paths leading to bus stops.

But once we entered the city, the architecture of czarist Russia proved more interesting, with pastel-colored buildings providing visual relief from the massive Soviet edifices. And as we neared Red Square, St. Basil's onion-shaped domes vibrantly countered the Kremlin's forbidding limestone walls.

Our hotel, the Intourist, was just off the square. It was, according to Desmond Smith, exclusively for foreign guests. The government did not want ordinary citizens mixing with foreigners in the airports so domestic lounges were separated from those used by foreigners.

After the check-in we had the first of numerous meals featuring tough meat of mysterious origin. The meals always included French fries, which became my main sustenance. Then came an inner-city tour, Anya pointing out the official monuments and buildings, Lilya pointing out the ones that Intourist didn't want us to know about, such as the pale-yellow home of the KGB.

We wandered Red Square, toured St. Basil's and stood in line for an hour or so to get a glimpse of Lenin in his tomb. Soldiers patrolled the line, making sure there were no cameras or other banned materials. Lenin looked remarkably good for someone dead for 50 years, good enough so that many Western experts believe that he is made from wax.

Each time we re-entered the hotel, we had to dodge a couple of teens wanting to purchase any blue jeans we might have or offering advantageous ruble/dollar exchange rates. A word or two from Anya and they would drift away. Off the hotel lobby there was a "dollar store" where foreigners could purchase Soviet souvenirs, but payment could only be made in U.S. dollars. There was also a bar, popular with late-night drinkers, that likewise only accepted dollars.

From those seeking jeans or dollars, there would be a hurried *nichevo* uttered as they scattered at Anya's admonition. Lilya explained that the word was the Russian equivalent of an accommodating shrug and the phrase "never mind." Muscovites, we learned, use the term several times daily – trying to complete a phone call, summoning an elevator, waiting for service from an indifferent waiter.

At our second meal in Moscow, facing another unidentifiable piece of meat, Helen looked at Marie, shrugged and muttered *nichevo*, much to our amusement and Anya's embarrassment.

After our introduction to Moscow's official Sovietdom, we boarded another Aeroflot Tupolev and headed south to Tbilisi, to the area that produced Josef Stalin. And where, according to journalist Hedrick Smith's knowledgeable account of his Soviet experiences, the Kremlin's hold had been severely compromised. Georgia, Smith reported, was home to entire off-the-books industries dedicated to producing black-market products destined for Moscow and Leningrad.

We were booked into the Tbilisi Hotel, an establishment on the far side of its glory days. High ceilings, marble staircases, room-size oil paintings – and an all-male dining-room band that could have graced the stage of a 1940s Hollywood movie. Each musician was outfitted in dark dress pants and starched white shirts. Upon learning that we were Americans, they broke into "Yankee Doodle" then followed up with "Melancholy Baby" featuring phonetic-English vocals.

Lilya's experience in Georgia was limited, but she compared it to "more like a sunny Mediterranean country" than the dreary and gray Moscow we had just witnessed. After our check-in, she and I took a walk around downtown. Within a block a boy of about 9 or 10 was following us, trying to flirt with Lilya. She confronted him with a torrent of Russian, sending him running – after he aimed a quick forearm-jerk insult at us, "just like it's done in Rome," Lilya noted.

On our walk, we noticed a flyer for a tennis event scheduled a couple of hours later. Featured were Billie Jean King and four other Americans, including John Lloyd, then married to Chrissie Everett. We decided we had to attend.

Back at the hotel, Lilya approached Anya about getting a couple of tickets for the pair of us. "Impossible," Anya said, noting that we were scheduled to attend the circus at the same time. Lilya then figured out where the tennis was taking place and how we could get there by bus. After arrival, we had no trouble purchasing tickets, even though the venue, a small indoor facility, only held about a thousand fans.

There, after the distraction of the metal-chair brawl on the landing behind us (quickly broken up by Soviet security), we were introduced to the character who would prove to be one of the journey's most interesting.

"In Moscow, just ask for Andrei the Great – everyone knows me there," he told us.

Lilya and I, seated about 20 rows up, had decided to try to make our presence known to the participating Americans. We yelled "Hey, John" at an appropriately quiet break in the action, assuming that was the last thing Lloyd would be expecting in Soviet Georgia. We were correct – he immediately turned in our direction and, spotting a cute blonde (that would be Lilya), he motioned us down. We were soon sitting with Lloyd (King was involved in her match), the American official in charge of the tour, and the Soviet translater/liaison/keeper, Andrei the Great.

The American official – I don't remember his name – was obviously taken with Lilya, but she was familiar with such attention and knew how to handle it. During a break in the action, Andrei and Mr. Official invited us back to the locker room for soft drinks. There, we got to know Andrei better.

He looked and sounded like Marty Allen, a Jewish comedian popular at the time: small of stature with an impressive Afro haircut and a distinctive Brooklyn accent. When I suggested that he must have spent time in New York to master English, he said that he had never been outside the Soviet Union and could not leave: "I'm still in trouble over my two divorces and three marriages," he explained with a grin.

Besides, he contended, he did not want to leave. "I love my country. If I don't like my job, I don't pay much attention to my duties, and they give me another job." Each comment was accompanied by a laugh.

Later, as Lilya and I returned to our hotel, she guessed that Andrei was KGB. The government, she said, would want the U.S. contingent closely watched while they were in the USSR so the apparatchiks would provide someone who spoke perfect English and therefore would be able to understand the meaning behind any probing questions. And any Russian with that kind of English expertise would have received the best training and education, the kind of training provided by the KGB.

When we neared our hotel rooms, Lilya noted that our floor lady was making a phone call – "She is telling Anya that we have returned," she said, adding with a smile, "Anya will now be able to relax and get a good night's sleep."

After Georgia, we flew east for Uzbekistan, with stops scheduled in Tashkent, Samarkand and Bokhara. Tashkent, the Soviet Union's fourth largest city at the time, had been the site of a devastating earthquake in 1966 and had been re-built with massive box-like Soviet edifices, official-looking and intimidating. If Tbilisi was more Mediterranean in culture and ambience, Tashkent, with its new buildings proudly utilitarian in their severity, was more a statement of the future as defined by official communism.

Laundry day in Uzbekistan

Our itinerary included show-off visits to a large center-city park, the country's largest statue of Lenin, and, in the evening, a ballet.

Lilya had told us that Tashkent was rumored to be the site of a notorious "thieves' market" where black-market goods were available. One item that supposedly could be found there was lapis lazuli, the semi-precious, intensely blue stone that has been mined in central Asia for centuries.

The next day, after Anya explained that "thieves' markets" were illegal in the Soviet Union and therefore did not exist, we were taken to a sprawling outdoor market.

Helen and Marie were looking for lapis lazuli, the rest of us just looking and taking a photo or two. At one point, as I haggled with a skull-capped man over a couple of small gourds that had been fashioned into snuff holders, the seller noticed that one member of our party was taking a picture. He immediately launched a gourd in the direction of the camera. We got the message.

After marveling at piles of melons and tastings of a sticky, grape-juice candy, we went back to the hotel for another meal only made palatable by the stiff shot of ice-cold vodka that served as the aperitif.

And then we were off to a lecture by local officials and a visiting dignitary. The subjects were economics and history. As we were discovering, the authoritative figures we encountered outside of Moscow were, invariably, posted from Moscow. The main speaker was such a figure. And, as a hedge against any slip-ups, his interpreter/translator was a Muscovite as well.

We were not the only English speakers in attendance, but the others were obviously on official business, with economics apparently the interest. At one point, after an inquiry delivered in Russian, the translator, with a surprised glance at the speaker that quickly turned into a pained stare, took the economist to task, while murmurs broke out among the Russian-speakers in the audience.

"Uh, oh – our speaker just made a mistake," Lilya whispered.

Finally, the translator responded with a muddled jumble of economic catch phrases that brought the lecture to an end. The question, Lilya explained as we prepared to leave, had been an inquiry about the paramount goal of the Soviet system. The answer, delivered forcefully by the economist: "We want to bury the United States." The translator told him he could not say that – and decided that was an excellent spot to end the talk.

After our check-in at the Samarkand Hotel in the centuries-old central Asian city, we got an irritating, *nichevo*-generating welcome. The elevator was not working and our rooms were on the seventh floor. Help with the bags for some of the older group was provided, but I chose to lug my stuff up the stairs. Slowed by my labors, I noticed that each step seemed to be a different height from the one before.

Setting my bags down, I took a closer look. Though I didn't try to measure them, it was obvious that there was plenty of variety. Did the height depend on which workman had that job on that day? Had the hotel been constructed by a crew involving Ivan Denisovitch Shukov's cadre? Or was it simply another example of the *nichevo* shrug?

Finally settled in my room, I watched as a windstorm hit the city, rust-colored dust blotting out the streets below. Through the centuries Samarkand has been the site of tyrannical raids by Mongol hordes and other ruthless invaders, and I was tempted to see the storm as an ominous sign.

At our first meal in Samarkand, Marie brought out her Polaroid camera. Pleased that he had American guests, the hotel manager was hovering around our table, ensuring that everything was suitable. After Marie asked him to smile for a picture, he watched in amazement as the photo emerged from the camera and his image – in color – slowly appeared.

Marie presented him with the picture and he soon was surrounded by his employees, marveling at this instant portrait.

Afterwards, he asked if we had any special meal requests. Our immediate answer was fresh vegetables or fruit.

At breakfast the next morning, each of us found a large bunch of grapes at our seat. And the manager introduced us to his wife. He had showed her his portrait and she had not believed him when he said he got it a minute or two after it was taken. So to convince her, he brought her to work. Naturally, Marie then took a picture of the two of them together. As hotel employees and restaurant guests passed the photo around we enjoyed our fresh grapes.

Unfortunately for most of us, me included, the grapes led to the Czars' Revenge. Dick, who was not affected, explained that the onslaught did not mean that we had food poisoning: "When your stomach is introduced to bacteria it hasn't encountered previously, it reacts by quickly sending it on. I guess that my stomach became familiar with that particular bacteria while I was living in India." He then generously shared from his cache of Pepto Bismol.

The next day we encountered Timur the Lame – aka Tamerlane – who is generally ranked in the top tier of history's ruthless conquerors, up there with Genghis Khan and Attila the Hun. Historians estimate that Timur was responsible for 17,000,000 deaths.

His demise in 1405 (while on the way to do battle with a Sino counterpart) was well-marked and his followers made sure he got a proper burial in his base of operations, Samarkand. In the early 1950s, the tomb, suitably grand for a despot of his fame, had drawn the attention of the Soviets and been spruced up to add credence to their claims of respect for the area's history.

So, after we had wondered at the splendors of the Bibi-Khanym mosque, one of Timur's signature projects, we were taken to his final resting place. Helen noted that she had never expected to be standing near the remains of a murderous despot, and then we got to talking about how we had come to Central Asia, in a part of the Soviet Union that was generally off-limits to Americans until officialdom's recent "thaw." I confessed that a movie had been my inspiration.

The film was "The Man Who Would Be King," based on a Rudyard Kipling story, directed by John Huston and starring Sean Connery and Michael Caine. The setting was Baluchistan, a sprawling mountainous site stretching over modern-day Afghanistan and Pakistan.

A trip to a travel agent led to the discovery that my best bet for seeing Central Asia was a 22-day tour of the Soviet Union. As bonus, I would spend time in Moscow, Leningrad and Siberia. At the time, I had only a vague notion of Tamerlane, an almost-mythic figure. Now, I was standing only a few feet away from his remains, resting under dirt and stone in a highly polished mausoleum.

Unhappy donkey in Tashkent

But, as our discussion continued, it was pointed out that given the reign of Josef Stalin, it was perhaps a despotic kinship that led to the restoration. Stalin's brutality, Helen noted, was responsible for an estimated 20,000,000 deaths.

Next stop after Samarkand was Bukhara, close enough so that Aeroflot opted for a propeller-driven airplane, their version of the work-horse DC-3 once common in the U.S. As with our other Aeroflot trips, the plane was at capacity.

The city, much smaller than Tashkent and Samarkand, seemed more rural in nature. Heaping piles of raw cotton were visible over the tops of walls as we were driven to official tourist sites. Cotton, Anya pointed out, is a primary product of the area, and would be transformed into the brightly colored textiles the area is known for. The textiles were popular with tourists from Eastern Europe and Russia seeking respite from their gray existence to the north and west.

Though the medresseh and mosques that are centuries-old now have been turned into museums they await much needed tilework restoration. They are still popular stops. As we had begun to notice, each now featured at least one elderly female stationed in each room, usually occupying a chair just inside the door. They were there, Lilya said, to keep an eye on us. And they all seemed to be entranced by the clothing worn by the women in our group – its Western style and bright colors in sharp contrast to the drab frumpiness of their attire.

In a small museum, the woman seated next to a highly polished samovar that occupied a place of pride took her eyes off Lilya's dress long enough to make sure that I understood I was not to take her picture. Once Lilya explained that I was only interested in the samovar, she grudgingly moved aside so I could get my picture. As a reminder of its history of brutal rulers, Bukhara's skyline was dominated by the Kelyan Minaret, built in the 12th century. In addition to its roles as an observation post and pulpit for calls to prayer, it had earned the nickname as the Tower of Death: Criminals and others out of favor with area rulers were thrown to their death from its top.

Other lingering images involve massive fortress walls still intact after a thousand years, and mosaics featuring Chinese dragons as well as Persian peacocks, visual testament to the city's importance as a stop on the ancient Silk Road. And, there's the image accompanying this fragment, a photo representative of what we were witnessing in 1977: an Uzbek leading his cow down an otherwise empty street, taken from the balcony of my room in a modern, multi-level hotel, this one featuring a working elevator.

Next up was a half-day's bus trip across the border into Tajikistan, the republic that provided the USSR a buffer from Afghanistan to the south and China to the east.

Intourist wanted us to see an archeological dig near the hamlet of Pendzhikent. Soviet scientists had dug around a centuries-old Zoriastrian site, but from all we could tell, the dig had not been active for decades. Weed infestation made the "attraction" anticlimactic, so we were driven back to Pendzhikent to visit a small museum.

Featured were a few ancient baubles, but what stood out to me was a display of graphic anti-Islamic propaganda: bloody images of torture and beheadings parroting the official Moscow take on the religion. Anya attempted an excusatory explanation, but since most of us were still having problems with the Czar's Revenge we were more interested in the museum's restrooms. And, for a change, at least a couple of the toilets were outfitted with seats.

The ride back to civilization included a stop at a roadside farm commune where female workers were harvesting potatoes and tobacco was drying on racks. Someone in our group noted that both products were new-world discoveries, which was news to Anya. But our visit was not a planned educational one – it was another bathroom stop.

By air, Eastern Uzbekistan to Irkutsk involves a flight of more than 3,000 miles – we would land in Tashkent and transfer from a small prop-jet to a larger craft. Simple enough in the U.S., but as we eventually learned, complicated in the Soviet Union. After deplaning at Tashkent's modern airport, we were ushered into the vast lounge set aside for foreign travelers, which we had to ourselves. Through a glass window we could see the much busier departure area for Soviet travelers, just below us.

As we waited to board the plane for our next leg – between trips to the bathroom – we played cards, we read, we talked with each other, we wondered what was taking so long. I decided to take advantage of the empty space to get some exercise by walking from end to end.

After much discussion, Lilya decided that she needed to visit the airport's clinic for help with her stomach problem. Her report back to us: "They decided I needed to eat more, which is the last thing I need to do. All I got was the typical *nichevo* response."

We played cards some more, we refined our grousing, Helen and Marie joined me in walking, introducing military-style cadence until the others let us know that we were no longer amusing. Anya, becoming more and more frustrated, would make periodic trips downstairs seeking information. Finally, someone mentioned that all our flights had been at capacity. And Lilya said, "that's it – they're waiting until every seat has been filled."

If she was correct – and she probably was – potential travelers were having too much fun in Tashkent to continue their journeys, postponing departure until the next day. We were taken back to the Tashkent Hotel – without our luggage – as the flight was rescheduled for the next day. Fortunately, since the hotel was new the toilets still had their seats.

The view from our jet was of miles of desert wasteland until we neared Kazakhstan's then-capital, Alma Ata, a re-fueling stop. We were now in the ancient homeland of the Sythes, one of the brutal nomad groups that dominated central Asia and had periodically threatened southern Europe in centuries past.

We had a couple of hours, so I decided to get outside the airport to try and appease my own nomadic yen by wandering around a bit. I managed to slip by Anya, but the airport was far removed from the rest of the city, so I didn't go far, settling for an unobstructed view of the Tien Shen Mountains. The range defines the border with China.

Eventually, the Czar's Revenge forced me back into the airport. But at least I could tell my friends that I had seen China, only admitting when pressed that it was from a couple of hundred miles away.

Late afternoon, we arrived in Irkutsk, unofficial capital of Siberia. A frontier atmosphere was dominant – wooden frame houses with firewood stacked outside, oxen-pulled work wagons on city streets, beat-up vehicles re-purposed as residences perched on high spots along the roiling Angara River and its tributaries. And the area's bloody Soviet history underlined that impression.

A re-purposed bus near the river in Irkutsk

Many of the Russians involved in the Decembrist Revolution of the early 1800s were exiled to the city, then more European Russians were sent there after the October revolution of 1917. During the latter, the area was the site of fierce battles between the Reds and the Whites.

We were domiciled at the Angara Hotel, an older downtown facility. Its location, I realized, would help in the daybreak excursions I was determined to make – I could easily walk to the shores of the Angara River a bit farther east.

At dinner, the hotel chef presented us with a welcome surprise – a golden aspic featuring a variety of mushrooms. Unfortunately, most of us could only nibble at it thanks to the wrathful grapes of Samarkand.

After dinner there was another circus, this one highlighted

by bears playing ice hockey. The crowd was more enthusiastic than the bears, but at least the action wasn't marred by chair-throwing fans like we had seen at the tennis matches in Tbilisi.

Daybreak the next morning I was at a bridge over a small tributary of the Angara shooting pictures when I noticed that the man who had been several yards behind me all the way from the hotel was loitering across the road, trying to look interested in the roiling water of the river.

The clip-clop of horses diverted my attention and I turned to be greeted by a friendly pair of Buryats on a wagon.

Then, as I realized breakfast time was near and I didn't want to face Anya's ire, I headed back to the hotel, my "escort" lagging a block or so behind.

Within a few hundred yards I heard a familiar sound – a female was leading an exercise group in a small park. A peek through the shrubbery revealed a dozen or so women working out to the recorded voice from a Soviet boom box. And the voice's familiarity made sense now that I could hear her clearly. It was a Jane Fonda tape.

After breakfast (and the disappearance of my "escort"), we undertook an hour-long drive the next day to a small settlement on the shore of Lake Baikal, the deepest and oldest in the world. There we toured a museum devoted to the lake's water residents, many of which are found only in Baikal.

Lunch – involving fish, of course – was in a modern facility overlooking the water.

Afterward, I attracted the attention of a goat, who followed me around as we checked out the wooden houses and their hand-carved frames and eaves. With snow swirling, the decision was made to return to Irkutsk. As I climbed back on board our bus, the nanny followed, finally being removed by the driver, her bleats sounding eerily like *nichevo*. The consensus of my fellow travelers was that she was attracted to my ragged beard.

We departed Irkutsk the next morning for Leningrad, our journey involving five time-zone changes, two refueling stops and a switch to a different jet in Moscow.

Our landing for fuel in Novosibirsk provided a scare. The jet – at passenger capacity, of course – taxied to the end of the runway, and turned to proceed to the terminal. Then the engines abruptly shut down. We sat and waited, and waited, and waited. There were nervous murmurs. Then someone noticed a fire truck headed in our direction with lights flashing. The murmurs became louder. Finally, Lilya got an explanation from a stewardess: The fire truck was needed to restart the jet engines. Soon, we were in the air again.

By the time of our visit to Leningrad, thanks to the persistence of the Czar's Revenge and the always-present Soviet atmosphere of repression and its resultant fear, I was looking forward to returning to the USA. But Leningrad provided a final ray of sun despite overcast skies.

Interestingly, after the collapse of the Soviet Union in the early 1990s, Russia was quick to return the city's pre-USSR name. St. Petersburg is much more suited to the city's Italian baroque architecture, its arts orientation, and, in 1977, its working, comparatively up-to-date facilities, many of which were built in Finland with a resultant Scandinavian-modern vibe.

We toured the Hermitage, with its rich collection of Impressionist paintings, and Petrodverets, the summer palace of Peter the Great with its tricked-up carousels. Our hotel was outfitted in Finnish-modern and overlooked the Aurora, the World War I ship that played a key role in the Bolshevik uprising that led to the establishment of the Soviet Union.

After a chance encounter with a poster touting a performance at the Kirov theater, Helen, Marie and I decided to see if we could obtain tickets. We were successful, but discovered that the staging was of "Eugene Onegin," a Tchaikovsky opera, instead of the ballet we thought we would be attending. But we had good seats, the theater was beautiful, and I assume the performance was up to par. It was my first operatic experience, so I won't venture a critique.

Before the opera began, I noticed a family in one of the private balcony boxes that included a girl of about 14. She was equipped with opera glasses and she had them trained on us. We synchronized a wave at her and were suitably rewarded with an embarrassed smile, then after whispers from her mother, the girl's binoculars were put away.

At intermission, we ventured from the auditorium in search of a drink – and found a charming custom from the past. There was a room set aside for promenading, with couples marching around, two by two, on a rectangular carpet as others watched and whispered among themselves. We assumed that the dress of the females was the primary topic.

Once we had returned to the hotel, I re-packed my bags,

climbed into bed and, looking forward to the return home, fell asleep. Then, only a few minutes later, I was jolted awake by loud explosions. After shaking the sleep-fog from my head, I looked out the window and discovered fireworks exploding over the Aurora. The city was celebrating a newly approved constitution, I learned at breakfast. But we interpreted the fireworks differently – they provided a suitable departure for us.

The next day Lilya and I took advantage of a two-hour refueling stop in Paris with a simple meal at an airport café. We agreed that the feast – a freshly baked baguette accompanied by a soft, flavorful cheese and cold Dutch beer – was the perfect welcome back to a world where such treats were normal.

EUROPE 1978

I know Brig, Switzerland only through a train window, only at night. Three times I have stopped there, entering and leaving Italy through the Semplon Pass, the route across the Alps developed by Napoleon. There my passport was checked, twice to make sure that I was fit for the ordered world of Switzerland, once to be welcomed to the relative chaos of Italy. All three times I was asleep upon arrival, waking because of the still silence. The window view was of serenity: empty platform, blue-cool glow from the station's lights, dark silhouettes of the mountains looming beyond.

The Semplon Pass, the after-midnight setting, the eerie silence – all mindful of a scene from a classic 1940s film, perhaps a romantic comedy. My second Brig stop, in the late 1970s, would have worked well in such a film. It involved a girl I had met on the platform at Florence, where we both were waiting for the same north-bound train, she headed home to Berne while I was in route to Paris. Nelli had spent a couple of months in the United States and was eager to practice her English. I was simply eager. The rail setting, of course, amplified the romance.

When I told Nelli that I had not seen the Matterhorn, she suggested we get off in Zermatt, pointing out that we could continue our voyages after a few hours. The next morning we were on the train for Berne. There, we said our good-byes and I continued to Paris, the city that always seems to be starring in a movie. After a couple of days in the Latin Quarter, with drinks at La Coupole underlining regrets about my stateside responsibilities, I continued to London for my flight back to the U.S.

My train traveling had begun in 1972, in Europe. There were memorable rail episodes in Germany, France and Spain. And, years later, in Australia and Mexico and the United States. There were friendly, fascinating companions, though they all paled in comparison to Nelli.

A Goodyear blimp over Rome

Spectacular scenery, high Alps to Australian Outback desert and Mexico's Barrancas del Cobre. Unexpected adventures, including witnessing a fistfight at a station in the Peloponnese and watching a troublemaker handcuffed on an Amtrak train in South Carolina. And I learned on three trips in Italy that dealing with rail lines in that country is always an adventure.

Since that 1972 journey, rail has been my favored way of getting from Point A to Point B, for many of the same reasons it has been favored by movie-makers: Diverse groups can be thrown together in a confined space; border crossings present opportunities for drama; interest builds easily as protagonists move farther and farther from the familiar.

Too, there are more mundane advantages: relaxation as someone else takes care of propelling you; the discovery of exotic cultures and locales; the sleep-inducing rhythm of the rails. And there is the excitement of heading into the unknown, a pleasure that can be made better at night when everything is in the abstract, lit up but only partially, mysterious shadows hiding pleasure and/or danger.

Early in my first foray to Europe, I discovered that I could sleep on overnight trains, saving the cost of a room. At that time most European trains featured compartments with bench seats that had room for three – if you were the only occupant there was plenty of space to stretch out and sleep. So it's 11 p.m. and you're in Hamburg and there's a train leaving for Vienna, due to arrive at 8 a.m.? Perfect, if you can find a compartment with plenty of space.

But I had booked a sleeper when I made my last stop in Brig in 2010, on my way home after herding a group of students around Cyprus for a month. Cramming as much travel as I could into my trip, I had spent several days in Milan before setting out for Paris, then, via the Chunnel, on to England for a Queen Mary voyage back to the U.S. The quiet Brig stop was a prelude to another movie scene, but it was more film noir than romance. There was no Nelli, just a female scream in the middle of the night.

At the time I had boarded around 11:30 p.m. I found that I was sharing a sleeper compartment with an Italian businessman who was a regular between Padua and Paris. He warned me that there was a lot of theft on the train, and since I was in the lower berth, I should make sure the door was locked.

After our passport-check in Brig, I was soon asleep. Then, about an hour into the Swiss Alps, I was awakened by the scream, followed, in English, by a female voice yelling "Stop, thief. You, get out." We could hear commotion in the corridor. Opting for caution, my compartment mate and I decided against opening the door to find out what was going on.

After a few minutes, and some animated chatter in Italian from the intruder and the conductor, it was determined that the woman had failed to lock her door, and another traveler, sleepily making his way back to his bed from the restroom, had mistakenly entered her compartment. Film noir comedy, perhaps.

Mexico 1981

In the early 1980s I took a job at *The Dallas Times Herald's* Sunday magazine, *Westward*. The paper was engaged in a circulation war with the *The Dallas Morning News*. It was a period when, as one report described it, the two papers were "throwing money at each other." And that meant we had resources for *Westward*. Interesting events taking place in Central America? Send a team down to cover them. Canadian financiers investing in prime downtown-Dallas real estate? Open a bureau in Toronto. How will the new Alaskan pipeline affect Texas oil and gas industry? Send a couple of staffers along with long-haul truckers.

So I wasn't surprised when my boss asked me one morning if I wanted to go to Mexico with our Pulitzer-winning photographer, Skeeter Hagler. We had sent a reporter to do a travel feature on the Barrancas del Cobre, a spectacular series of canyons in the Sierra Madre Occidental. And now we needed photos. Skeeter's Pulitzer provided him with enough pull to insist that he needed someone to accompany him. And I had never been to Mexico – enough reason in my mind to take the four-day trip.

Southwest Airlines to El Paso, a taxi to the border, another taxi to Juarez, then a train to Chihuahua, where we would spend the night before catching the <u>Ferrocarril Chihuahua al Pacífico,</u> otherwise known, we quickly learned, as the Chepe. The first Mexican leg of the journey provided a proper introduction when we stopped in the middle of nowhere. There was a northbound train, also stopped, on the tracks alongside us. We joined our fellow passengers in watching a quartet of uniformed federalistas dis-embark, their objective apparently to board our train. The fourth federalista brought a roar of laughter from the passengers when he fell as he got off.

One of our car-mates explained that the soldiers would come through on a shake-down walk, seeking bribes. Skeeter and I were assured that we would not be bothered since we were from north of the border and were carrying press identification. We then watched as a couple of the federalistas prodded the packages carried by their fellow countrymen, generally hassling anyone who they didn't like or who looked like they might be "smuggling" something of value purchased in El Paso.

Asleep on the Chepe, captured by Skeeter

The Mexicans glared at them, or, in a couple of cases, barely suppressed laughter when the soldier who had taken the fall tried to act tough. Later, we were told that our presence had blunted the bribery efforts.

In Chihuahua we grabbed burritos at a downtown café and watched the traditional late-afternoon promenade around the otherwise sleepy downtown square, then turned in.

An optimal run of the Chepe is scheduled at 12 hours, but often takes 14 or 15. There are scheduled stops with grand views, smoke from Tarahumara fires visible on the bottom of the canyons. But there are also unscheduled delays.

Early the next morning we were aboard the Chepe. Within a couple of hours, we were climbing, vistas becoming more and more spectacular. At Dividisero, there was a 20-minute photo stop where we were introduced to the native Tarahumara, famous for their long-distance running and their peyote-centered religion. Several were offering their wood carvings and baskets for sale, their presence ensuring great photos for Skeeter Hagler.

About midnight we had just begun our descent from the heights when there was a halt at a small village. Skeeter and I were in the last car, Skeeter napping as I hung out at the open end of the back with a drunk native. Periodically, his friend the conductor would admonish him to be quiet, to sit down, to quit causing trouble. He would look at me and laugh.

When we stopped, the conductor exited the car at the other end with his signal light. And the drunk exited at our end to relieve himself. After a couple of minutes I glanced toward the conductor and saw him waving the light that meant we were ready to continue. I alerted my "friend". My voice got the conductor's attention, and when he saw what was going on he started yelling at the drunk, whose response was loud laughter. As the train started slowly moving, he finished his business and started running for the train. I reached down, grabbed his arm and pulled him aboard.

"Gracias, amigo," he said, grinning at me as the conductor arrived and started marching him back down the car. Looking into the canyon I could see the faraway lights of Tarahumara fires, only then realizing that if my "friend" had been stronger, I could be tumbling down the mountain to join them.

After recovering from our 16-hour train trip, Skeeter and I decided to wait a day in Los Mochis before making the return trip to Chihuahua. Skeeter wanted images of the train as it pulled into its first stop on the return. So, after a confusing 15 minutes with a group of taxi drivers whose lack of English-language skills were on a level with our lack of Spanish-language expertise, we hired a taxi. We tried to explain that we wanted to get ahead of the train for a shot of the locomotive coming toward us, while our driver thought we wanted to catch the train. Finally, the hotel's desk clerk translated, explaining our intentions.

After a couple of in-vain treks down muddy roads, the driver dodging naked children splashing in the puddles, we finally got what we wanted. But now we had the rest of the day to see what else we could find. We somehow convinced our driver to get us to a spot where we could see the Sea of Cortez, and that meant Topolobampo, a small port with ferry service to Cabo San Lucas. A schedule check revealed that we could not cross and return in time to catch the next day's Chepe, so we pointed to a church steeple on top of a near-by hill. Our driver, now resigned to the fact that we were not the usual pliant tourists, reluctantly agreed to take us there.

At the hill's top, there was a plaza fronting the church with several photogenic children at play. But as Skeeter took pictures, our driver noticed that one of his taxi's tires was low. With a look of panic, he told us we had to go. We tried to tell him to go get it fixed and then come back for us. With a determined "No, senor. Go, go" he pushed us into the back seat.

Safely back in our hotel, we told the clerk what had happened. And he explained that Topolobampo, as a main port on the gulf, was popular with drug smugglers shipping their goods to Cabo and to Tijuana. "It is not a place to be with expensive cameras," he said.

The next morning we boarded the Chepe for the return to Chihuahua. Running late because of our train-chasing, we chose to fly from Chihuahua back to the states. Plus, as Skeeter pointed out, in the air we would not have to risk another attempted federalista shake-down.

Chilé 1981

Shortly after I arrived back in the office following my long weekend in Mexico, the paper's travel editor, Michael Carlton, walked in. "Want to go to Chilé?" he asked. My "yes" was immediate, and was quickly followed by a "when?" I was told I would leave in two weeks and would be gone for eight days.

I crammed two weeks' worth of work into the next six days so that I could be absent the following week. Then I flew to Miami to meet with Pan American Airline's representative and the other eight members of an invited group for a flight to Santiago. And that's how I was introduced to travel-writers' junketing.

I would discover that Pan American's Lou Hammond was expert at leading such groups – no matter how late and how spirited the previous evening's partying, she was always on time and wide awake at the next morning's breakfast. And she was expert at sidestepping special requests from junket participants. Carlton had told me that she was the best – and that it would be to my benefit to stay on her good side.

"She is," he said, "THE person to know when it comes to travel to exotic places."

Pan Am was re-inaugurating service to Chilé and was co-sponsoring the trip with Holiday Inn, which had recently opened luxury hotels in Santiago. The Chiléan government's travel bureau had also signed on.

Our first couple of days were spent in Santiago, where there was a noticeable military presence. Auguste Pinochet had recently consolidated his power with a new constitution naming him president, and it seemed that every downtown street corner featured three or four heavily armed soldiers.

Our first official visit was to the offices of a leading Santiago newspaper, where the editor cheerfully admitted that his publication supported Pinochet's government despite its burgeoning reputation for corruption and pro-military brutality.

As our questions became more probing, our official local guide hustled us out for our next stop, a winery. Plentiful samples of the excellent Cabernet Sauvignon produced in the area's Maipo Valley quickly put us into a more friendly mood. Then it was lunch at a Bavarian restaurant in a town just south of Santiago that was settled in the mid-1800s by Germans lured to Chilé by government emissaries seeking settlers.

But the next day we would be exposed to a more personal Pinochet-government experience on our way to Valparaiso and its adjoining seaside resort, Vina del Mar. Led by our official guide, we were aboard our own small bus when we were stopped at a military checkpoint. Despite our leader's protests, we were ordered to disembark and produce our passports while a couple of the soldiers checked the inside of the bus.

Finally, the officer in charge smugly smiled and allowed us back on the bus. As our guide silently seethed, we proceeded to Vina del Mar, our trip to the beach and its casino soured by our experience.

Just outside our hotel the next morning I noticed a couple of skiers boarding a bus labeled Portillo. The resort is one of the world's top ski destinations and though I'm certainly not skilled enough to be frequenting such slopes, my face lit up enough to catch Lou Hammond's eye. She sighed and reminded me that skiing would not be part of this trip, but she promised plenty of excitement anyway. "We'll be going south tomorrow, to Patagonia," she pointed out. Mindful of Carlton's advice and of Pan American's position in international air travel, I smiled and agreed that Patagonia would be fascinating.

After a night consuming the national brandy, pisco, and trying to compete with dance-crazy Chiléans at a supper club, the next morning we blearily boarded a flight for Puerto Montt. We would travel 600 miles down the coast to the last jump-off spot for Chilés extreme south. The flight was spectacular enough to keep me awake – snow-covered Andes on the left, blue Pacific on the right.

My recollections of Porto Montt are of a sleepy fishing village, a wooden dock featuring bountiful and delicious oysters on the half shell and sea urchins served in their own salty liquid. And of Osorno, the nearby volcano. Today, a half-century later, Puerto Montt is a city of more than 250,000 and the center of salmon farming, but Osorno is still the major presence.

After delicious oysters consumed at a ramshackle, on-the-water café, we headed east toward Osorno and the glacial lakes district, for the waterfalls of Saltos del Petrohue on to Ralun and a friendly neighbor who passed by our lodge on horseback, wielding a scythe, in route to his fields.

Afterwards, along the shore of the Reloncavi fjord, we spent a couple of days of luxury in the middle of a primitive farming and fishing area – dirt roads, wood-fire heat, and hearty meals. After a short horseback trip on the shores, the entertainment consisted of snooker on a Victorian-era table. And the remote site gave us an excellent opportunity for viewing the southern hemisphere's night, with its new-to-me constellations. Our host was Raymond Lechner Duncan, whose family background (German and Scotch) is typical of the country, especially the agriculture centers of the south, where vast *estancias* are home to thousands of sheep.

In fact, Chilé is a mix of many nationalities and cultures, from the native Araucanian to folks from all over Europe. The

Irish played prominent roles: The father of Chilé was Bernardo O'Higgins, who led the war of independence from Spain, and the founder of the country's navy was named Cochrane. But other backgrounds continually made their presence known. One of our guides was a second-generation Italian named Dioghero and our driver in Santiago was descended from Eastern European Jews. In the far south, the language you'll hear is as likely to be Slavic as Spanish.

And there were Americans, too. Pinochet's economic policy was borrowed from the so-called Chicago Boys, proponents of Milton Friedman's free-market ideology.

But another American stands out in my memory. Daryle Ryce was the star of our hotel's cocktail lounge in Santiago. Ms. Ryce is Black, a songwriter and singer who accompanied herself on piano. Booked into the hotel for six months, she had made the lounge one of the city's most in-demand attractions. In a brief conversation during a break, she admitted to being somewhat homesick. And, with a nod toward our table, she closed her show with a heart-felt "Blues for the Folks Back Home."

When I began this memoir, I discovered that Ms. Ryce is still singing professionally, a regular at a spot in her hometown of Landrum, in South Carolina's Piedmont. There the mountains are much smaller – and perhaps more comforting – than the knife-edged peaks that tower over Santiago.

Australia 1981

The Aussies crowded into the roadhouse were drunk and unruly, pushing and shoving as they fought for position in front of the stage. Perhaps the mood was appropriate considering the star. Eric Burden became famous as the leader of the Animals, an English top-40 group in the late '60s known for blues-tinged songs delivered in a raucous, in-your-face manner.

Though the Animals made their mark a decade earlier, Burden still had a following in Australia in 1981. Before the band had even made it on to the stage, I witnessed two fist fights in the crowd.

I was in Australia on a two-week travel-writing junket with four other writers and our guide. But I had I made the trip to the show alone – none of my fellow travelers were interested in joining me on a trip to a sketchy area on the outskirts of the city.

I was there because on the hotel elevator that morning I had noticed that the English being spoken by the two men already on board was of the American variety. It turned out they were from Houston and were part of Burden's band. And they invited me to the night's performance with comp tickets. I am a Burden fan, so I told them I would be there.

A long taxi-ride later I was clutching my beer and trying to hold my position a few feet in front of the stage. There were tables, but the large crowd meant standing-room-only in most of the room.

Burden and band were in fine form, but the crush made it difficult to hold both my position and my beer. Plus there was a fog of cigarette smoke, so at intermission I escaped outside for air. In the parking lot I discovered more Aussies, many of them seated on the hoods of automobiles and trucks facing the screen of the drive-in movie theater that backed up to the parking lot. On the screen were large-scale images of female nudity – the night's feature was soft-core pornography.

The movie meant that the crowd inside thinned somewhat during the band's second-half performance and I was able to find a table seat to enjoy the show without having to fend off drunks.

The next morning I met my new friends – and Burden – in the hotel lobby as they were departing. I told them how much I had enjoyed the music. And Burden said, "I'm glad somebody did, because apparently a lot of the Aussies didn't – they didn't come back after intermission."

I explained about the movie next door, and they laughed. "That's a relief," Burden said. "That'll make our flight to Perth more pleasant."

Then they wanted to know where I was headed. When I told them Alice Springs, one of the Houston pair told me with a grin: "The joints in Alice are like the chicken-wire places in Texas."

Answering Burden's quizzical look, he explained. "At Texas roadhouses the crowds can get downright dangerous, so they put up chicken-wire screens to protect the band from thrown beer bottles." Burden shook his head and chuckled. We swapped "good-luck" wishes, they departed for Australia's western coast, and I went upstairs to pack for our flight to the next stop, Kangaroo Island off the coast from Adelaide. The island is rich with its namesake, but sheep far outnumber both native species and their two-legged owners, we were informed by our host.

Rex Ellis would serve as our guide on the island and provide us with our means to cover its acreage – he runs camel safaris both on the island and in the Simpson Desert between Adelaide and Alice Springs on the Australian mainland.

Ellis is as much a naturalist as an entrepreneur, his quiet confidence reflected in his ease with ignorant tourists.

Leading us through the bush to the edge of the island's spectacular coastal bluffs, he assured us there was no need to worry about our steeds. They are, he noted, more sure-footed than goats and a hell of a lot easier to ride.

I spent most of a day astride my camel trying to ignore the flies gathered around my head and back, only the netting on my hat saving me from their bites.

When one member of the group suggested a small, intimate beach for our lunch-stop, Ellis quickly added a note of reality. After pointing out the seals lying in the sand, he said, "Where there are seals, there are sharks, and these waters are home to Great Whites."

A few hours later at Port Arthur, we boarded The Ghan, Trans-Australian Railway's fabled line that crosses the Simpson Desert. On the train, I learned that the name is derived from its connection to Afghanistan, and that in turn explains the feral camels sometimes spotted on the voyage. The railway was constructed around the turn of the last century by builders who had honed their skills working on lines in central Asia. Camels and their Afghan keepers had been imported to provide desert expertise.

Our compartments on the Ghan were luxurious:

lovingly polished wood, elegant brass fittings, plush upholstery fabrics. But the scenery was desert, and after I had tired of trying to spot a feral camel or two, my night with the musical Animal – Eric Burden – caught up with me and I fell asleep, lulled by the rhythm of the rails.

In Alice the next afternoon, with our escort, Hella, leading the way, we picked out a likely looking pub. The ambiance, both of the fixtures and the grizzled male-only drinkers – was that of rough-and-tumbled American Old West. Hella quickly noticed a sign above the entry into an adjoining room that said "Ladies".

When the bartender suggested we might be more comfortable in that room, her withering glance prompted a quick backpedal: "But you're welcome to stay in here." Looks from the other customers belied his words, but after a glance or two at us they returned to their previous conversations.

But in 1981 efforts were being made to modernize Alice, using another desert oasis, Las Vegas, as inspiration. A glitzy new Federal Casino had been opened, complete with lots of neon, noisy slot machines and a flashy floor show. The scale

Friendly Cockatoo near Hanging Rock

was smaller than what's typical for Vegas: where the clubs in Nevada might feature a dozen scantily clad chorines, in Alice there were only three. But the show's featured singer, a native of Bali, did pull off a phonetic feat, closing his set with "MacArthur Park," Jimmy Webb's mysterious, complex anthem of the 1960s.

Petroglyphs near Alice Springs

Next on the agenda was Ayers Rock, in the desert a short flight south of Alice. Our rudimentary lodging consisted of a collection of pre-fab single-story buildings that had been trucked in and assembled around a small swimming pool. It would be a couple of years before Australia turned the rock over to its aboriginal residents, who restored the rock's name, Uluru, and built a first-class resort a few miles north.

Settling into my room, trying out the bed, I had a bit of a scare. There was a spider clinging to the wall a couple of feet above my head. It was light brown in color and not tarantula-hairy – but it was larger than my hand and I was in a place foreign to me. So I carefully exited the bed and hurried to the hotel office/bar/poolroom for information.

After I described my arachnid roommate to Jacky, the bartender, he grinned. "It's harmless, mate. But watch out for light-brown snakes." Then he poured me a Foster's beer and we became acquainted. Pointing to one of the men at the pool table, he explained. "Slim over there's an expert on brown snakes. Lost a mate to one. They're deadly."

Our Outback visit continued with a tour of the Uluru area, to the Olga Mountains, to ancient petroglyphs, to fleeting glimpses of cowboys who have opted for motor bikes instead of horses as they search for stray livestock.

Our next overnight stop was the Ross River ranch of Gil Green a few miles northwest of Alice. At Gil's you will find working cowboys, uncloudy skies and few discouraging words, unless you happen to be around when one of the locals has to help a "bloody stupid" tourist who has ignored the sign warning of quicksand and ventured into a seemingly dry stream bed.

The Outback visit provided a suitable wrap for our two weeks. The Aussie attitude, the droll, laid-back approach to whatever came along, was intensified by the stark desert landscape, perhaps best exemplified by Uluru's incongruous presence. Such a landscape seemed to attract those with a tough-edged acceptance of whatever life threw at them, those who would take a desert confrontation with a camel in stride, those who would ignore casino glitz in favor of billiards in a dusty Alice Springs bar where women were expected to keep to their own designated space. When he had guests, Gil Green provided a handy example at his cozy ranch bar, turning day-to-day problems into late-afternoon drolleries of Outback follies delivered laconically over bottles of ice cold beer.

The camaraderie and cool refreshment hinted at English high tea – but with a distinctive Australian twist.

Israel 1982

On June 6, 1982, the Israeli military invaded Lebanon, to attack the Phalangists, which started a conflict that lasted for several months and left approximately 20,000 people dead.

Four days later I exited a TWA jet at David Ben-Gurion Airport outside Tel Aviv. But I wasn't there to cover the war – I was part of a group of travel writers in a week-long junket, visiting many of the most popular tourist stops in the history-rich area.

I was a veteran of travel and of writing about it. But this was my first visit to a country that was at war. At the time I was working for a Dallas magazine and had gotten an invitation a month or so earlier from the Israeli consulate in Houston. Besides the handful of writers, our group included a dozen or so travel agents from around the U.S. – so I assume that the Israeli tourism department was not privy to the military's plans.

Our journalist convoy was large enough – with a dozen small rental sedans, four travelers assigned to each – so that we formed our own parade. My traveling companions consisted of a reporter from Fort Worth, a freelance writer from Raleigh, N.C. and her friend, a photographer from Miami, the pair on assignment for a New Jersey newspaper. Our week-long visit would include sites holy to Jews, Muslims, and Christians; an over-night in a kibbutz guest house; futile attempts to submerge ourselves in the Dead Sea; a walk over sections of the Via Dolorosa to the Church of the Holy Sepulcher; through-the-glass views of what's left of the Dead Sea scrolls; and a sobering visit to the Holocaust memorial.

We soon realized that hitch-hiking soldiers in uniform expected to be given rides by civilians. And the soldiers we encountered – male and female – were well armed. We picked up a black Beta Israelite on the road to Jerusalem. Abraham Chekole was born in Ethiopia and had lived in Germany and Sudan before 1977, when the Israeli government decided that members of the Ethiopian community, then known as Falashans, were in fact descendants of one of the 12 tribes of Israel and therefore should be included in the Law of Return.

Troop carriers moving north of Tel Aviv toward Lebanon

That decision meant that our passenger could emigrate to Israel and become a citizen. Abraham's English was excellent and he was willing to answer questions about his presence, though he was circumspect about his current military role, describing his recent activity as "playing ping-pong" in Lebanon. As to his faith, he said he believed in God but did not embrace organized religion. Our passenger exited in Jerusalem in favor of a military convoy headed north, to re-join his unit and continue his "ping-pong" activity. Our next stop was at a gas station. The Palestinian proprietor reluctantly responded to our questions about his situation with "too much fighting – all the time is war."

Though such encounters were reminders of how close we were to the fighting, other activity indicated how war is a "normal" part of life in Israel. At another highway stop, we helped two nuns as they struggled with a flat tire on their Peugeot, after which they invited us to visit their hospice on Mount Beatitudes. They did not mention the nearby battles, seemingly oblivious to the war.

The conflict was more evident on the Mediterranean coast, where tanks and soldiers carrying weapons were difficult to ignore. As we drove north from Tel Aviv, fighter jets off to our left screamed toward the seaside cliffs that define the border.

Military helicopters were always in evidence, transporting troops and arms up and down the coast. At one stop we waited as a convoy moved toward the front, residents tossing oranges up to the soldiers aboard troop carriers and tanks.

As we drew closer to our destination, the beach resort of Nahariyya, we realized that the booms we were hearing resulted from the bombs striking just inside Lebanon, only a few minutes away. Each time we heard a boom, we could watch the ensuing cloud of smoke.

After an anxious lunch, we hurried to Haifa, midway between the border and Tel Aviv. There, we had the opportunity to ensure that our memory stayed with us. Colorful t-shirts bearing the military's designated shibboleth for the operation, Peace for Galilee, were offered for purchase.

After our first couple of days of travel in-country, and the reminders that we were in a war zone, we drove through Nazareth to the Sea of Galilee and the city of Tiberias. We would spend that night in Kibbutzim guest houses, center of a 2,500-acre farm community where cooperation and sharing are primary – "toiling the Holy Land" we are told.

The next day, my car-mates and I determined that our best chance of experiencing Israel in the broadest sense was to hang back at the end of our convoy. Generally, one of our handlers piloted the tail-end car, but we had discovered that the presence of photographer Len Kaufmann in our car meant that we had a legitimate reason to stray for photo ops.

At one point after we left the Kibbutzim, we spotted what appeared to be the ruins of a village on a hillside off to our right. We detoured up to it and discovered a Bedouin encampment within the mud-brick walls of an abandoned refugee camp.

The ruins provided an easy way for the nomads to keep their goats in one place as well as wind-shelter for their tents. The ancient Bedouin lifestyle provided us with another example of the necessity of community in the harsh Middle Eastern climate.

But while the Israelis had welcomed us to their Kibbutz, the Bedu weren't too pleased with our intrusion. Their dogs made sure we did not linger around to take photos – we were soon hurrying to catch up to our official convoy as it headed south for our next overnight stop, a resort on the Dead Sea.

After we had attempted to submerge in the salt-heavy water, and lengthy showering to get rid of the salt, we headed to Masada, about 20 miles west. The 2,000-year-old site of the massive fortress built by Herod is atop a mesa, and is one of the richest archeological areas in the Middle East. The city that was built around the fortress was excavated in the early 1960s, yielding a trove of facilities and implements of everyday life during the first centuries after the birth of Christ.

There are palaces, ritual baths, a synagogue, villas as well as cave dwellings, a system for the reservoir of water, hundreds of rooms designed for storage of everything from grain to arms – necessities in case of a siege.

Since the site's excavation, Masada routinely ranks second to Jerusalem in popularity with Israel's tourists. We are among several hundred tourists wandering around the 18-acre site.

After an hour or so listening to the drone of academics outlining the virtues of the ancients, made worse by the intensity of the mid-day sun, we decide to descend to the air-conditioned refuge of our hotel. There, over cold drinks, we realize that we have a free evening and decide to experience modern-day life in ancient Palestine.

And Arad, about 20 miles to the southwest, looked like the perfect place. As one of Israel's first planned cities, Arad became the new home of many of the Jews who immigrated from the Soviet Union in the 1970s. There, we reason, we can get a feel for today's Israel, miles away from the war's front.

We find what we are looking for – comfortable seating, cold drinks and a relaxed meal at a sidewalk café in a bustling, modern downtown. We spend an hour or so without any of what had become the tour's standard "brief remarks" extolling Israel's virtues for tourists.

The break came at a welcome time – the night before we had listened to an official's quarter-hour diatribe about what he characterized as the U.S. media's bias against Israel. Even our handlers had been embarrassed by his "remarks."

Finally, around 9 p.m., we decide it is time to drive back to our Dead Sea hotel. We have the road to ourselves until we close on taillights ahead. The lights, we quickly discover, belong to an armored truck equipped with a long-range cannon. We suddenly are blinded by large spotlights on the rear of the vehicle, lights that are pointed at us. As the truck rolls to a halt, we do, too.

Soldiers then examine our papers and listen to our story. Next, they escort us to our hotel, their presence reminding us that in Israel, we are never far from the front.

With a group of armed female soldiers at a miniature Bethlehem display in Jerusaleum

Photo by Len Kaufmann

GOOFS, GAMBITS
& OTHER MISCHIEFS

A cardigan sweater, Wyoming grits, Flannery O'Connor, mischievous cats, and Big Red who went to Minnesota and died. Plus, a brief appearance by one of Cormac McCarthy's most memorable creations.

I was introduced to newsroom mischief during my first week of work at *The Knoxville Journal*. I was 19 years old, nervous about my first real job, hustling to make sure that I did not lose it. The year was 1965.

One of my duties involved periodically collecting copy from various departments – from the city desk, from the society editor, from the photography office, from chief editor Guy Lincoln Smith, from the top of a file cabinet that divided the sports department from the city-side reporters. Deliveries would then be made to the news desk, to the engraving department, sometimes to a particular editor on the other side of the newsroom.

When I started my duties typewriters were our word processors and carbon paper was our way of creating duplicates. On a particular afternoon of that first week, I had grabbed a couple of stories from the sports-department tray, and promptly slipped on a sheet of carbon paper and landed on my butt. Grady Amann, one of the editors in sports, jumped up, pointed at me as I struggled to right myself and shouted, "Hey, no dancing."

Within a couple of months I knew that Grady was only one of a half-dozen dedicated pranksters in *The Journal* newsroom, that one of the more popular "games" was slipping off-color comments into print, and that a couple of the more serious employees were the victims-of-choice. There was the wire editor who kept several decks of cards in a desk drawer for games of Solitaire when things were slow. I don't think he ever discovered that his co-workers had removed one card from each deck, ensuring constant defeat.

The Journal was a morning newspaper, which meant that most of the editors worked at night. When I began, I punched in at 2 p.m. and my shift ended at 11. Later, my hours were 5 p.m. to 2 a.m. The top editors went home at 5 p.m.; the mid-level editors left at 9 p.m. Those of us who worked late frequently had time for plotting, for welcoming female friends bearing cold beer into our domain, and then composing stories involving them. A couple of times "doctored" front pages with mentions of our chums were made so we could pull proofs with the names of girlfriends included. The stories would then be destroyed. On one occasion I covered a beauty pageant in a nearby town that featured a female friend, who insisted that her mother had forced her to enter. The story ran in the edition that she and her family saw, then I pulled it before the City edition, which my bosses would be checking. They never knew of its publication, but my friend would not speak to me for a couple of weeks.

By the time I had moved from the *Journal* to *The Miami Herald*, also a morning paper but with a much larger staff, I was well-versed in newsroom pranks. *The Herald* was not the place for inserting personal "news" stories, but there was plenty of late-night mischief. There was the copy boy who supplemented his salary by selling marijuana to his co-workers – he was found out when an accident left his product scattered around the floor of the wire-room. There was the late-night editor who posted a copy-machine rendition of his butt on an office bulletin board.

And there was the reaction to an edict from on-high limiting each reporter to one file cabinet for clips and notes. The reporter whose hoarding had led to the new rule brought heavy chains and locks into the office, waited until the bosses had gone for the day and chained the extra cabinet to the support column next to his desk.

After *The Herald*, I worked at one more morning newspaper, *The Charlotte Observer*, before moving to afternoon publications and positions that involved more reasonable working hours. For some of us, our more creative endeavors morphed into using odd incidents encountered in legitimate stories as starting points for attempts at fiction. Our motive was delusional – one spell-binding novel would bring freedom from newspaper drudgery.

The Goofs, Gambits & Other Mischiefs section includes several examples of such efforts. There are send-ups to the traditional heart-warming Christmas-holiday story, a couple of take-offs on incidents that occurred when I was writing travel stories, and there is the section devoted to Carl LaFong, the handle I gave to my music-reviewing alter ego when I worked as an editor at *The Dallas Times Herald* in the early 1980s.

LaFong (the name borrowed from a W.C. Fields movie) became infamous in the Dallas newsroom after artist and page designer James Noel Smith, my talented cohort (and fellow East Tennessee native) decided to give him a "look." When I questioned his rendering – scraggly beard and unkempt hair – he argued that LaFong should have a "what the hell?" attitude.

Carl LaFong became my pseudonym of choice when I needed one. And James Noel supplied other quick sketches – a couple of examples are included as part of this section.

Months later, my alter ego had made enough of an impression to garner interest from one of the Houston newspaper editors, who was looking for a new popular-music writer. At a Sunday-magazine gathering, James Noel and I were joined at lunch by the Houston editor. He told us he had noticed LaFong's work and wanted to talk to him about the possibility of a job in his features section.

James Noel and I had a good laugh at the editor's expense and then confessed that I was LaFong and had no desire to relocate to Houston. Eventually I abandoned the pseudonymous alter ego, though he still lives on as a joke among my friends.

Though his name was not used, LaFong's spirit was evident in the printed result of an idea that I had in 1988. The subject was a group of absurd "moments" in the South's past. I created the ideas and captions and James Noel provided drawings. I mentioned the project to Jim Morgan, the editorial director of *Southern* magazine, and he suggested that I send them along. Morgan used three to create a two-page spread under the title "Little Known Chapters in Southern History." One of the three later was reprinted by Malcolm Jones in Florida's *St. Petersburg Times*. Those three are reproduced here.

After we created "Westwords" as a column in the Sunday magazine, we were soon publishing work by some of Dallas' best essayists. But occasionally a piece would fall through at the last minute. Usually we had a backup that we could use. But one Friday (deadline day) in the spring of 1981, we were faced with an empty folder.

So I resurrected LaFong for a piece about a character I had known growing up in Knoxville, a hillbilly whose surname was Yarber. His story kicks off this section, a grouping of other characters encountered in other places.

The junior high school I attended in Knoxville, Tennessee, wasn't one of those big-city, junkyard-mean ghetto places, but only because it wasn't big. In the late 1950s when I entered the seventh grade, it was certainly trying:

There was enough skullduggery that the *Black and Gold*, the mimeographed school newspaper, could justify publishing a "Crimes" column. One example involved a student named Lester, who ran a "protection" racket modeled on the ones he'd seen in the movies. He had three or four henchman who provided muscle.

Lester and one or two of his pals would approach an innocent 12-year-old. "Look, kid, what would you do if somebody just walks up to you and gives you a knuckle sandwich?" he would ask.

"Huh?" (Seventh graders aren't known for quick perception).

"You know, what if someone hauled off and slugged you when you were leaving the wood shop?"

"Oh. Why would someone do that?"

"Look, kid, if you'll pay us a dime a week, my boys will see to it that no one, and I mean NO ONE, does anything to bother you."

Of course, if the kid balked he would catch a black eye on his way to his next class. Lester must have been successful. He was the only seventh grader at school who had a car. Word on the playground was that he had been a seventh grader for three years.

His car was a gray-primered 1953 Mercury and was envied by everyone except Sanford, who had a motorcycle, was 18 and had made it to the eighth grade.

Lester's chief enforcer was named Harrison. Everyone knew that Harrison carried a switchblade, although no one had actually seen it. He got the job after Lester's chief muscle was arrested during home group one morning. For burglary.

Every crime boss has to have a clown accomplice, and Lester had chosen well. Yarber was small of stature, but he tried to compensate with a carefully cultivated ducktail haircut and stove-pipe pants. But most of the time his tough-guy efforts would be overcome by his lack of good sense.

Yarber was the planner, executor, and ultimately, the pigeon in the Great Birdbath Heist. After deciding he needed a birdbath, Yarber convinced two other members of Lester's outfit to lend a hand. The particular model he fancied belonged to the family of a girl at school. She was a model student, outstanding piano player, cheerleader, budding beauty queen, and disdainful of anyone who sported a ducktail. And she was the star of Yarber's secret dreams.

On the night in question, Yarber grabbed the "bowl" half of the bath, his cohorts grabbed the base and they ran, or tried to run. After they had gone only a few feet, the porch light came on and the girl's father stepped to the door.

Yarber's partners dropped their half and made good their escape. Yarber, however, refused to turn loose of his part and, struggling like a madman, was caught. Fortunately, the girl persuaded her father that it was all a harmless prank and Yarber should be turned loose. Word of the attempted heist spread and thereafter Yarber was known as Birdbath.

He could have been called Cherry Bomb, after the firecrackers of choice at Park Junior. Their waterproof fuses meant that they could be lit, dropped into a toilet which would then be flushed. The resultant flood would, optimally, bring an early end to the day's classes. Lester and his gang were always suspect when this happened but school officials were never able to pin the crime on them. Until Yarber inadvertently blew the case open.

After a particularly nasty explosion and flood, Lester slipped his Cherry Bomb inventory into Yarber's locker for safekeeping. The next day Yarber was catching a quick smoke at his locker when a teacher rounded the corner, headed his way. Ever cool, Yarber casually laid the cigarette on the locker shelf, closed the door and sauntered down the hall. The explosion moved Yarber's locker and five adjoining ones off the wall and sent the teacher into early retirement.

But Yarber's real moment of glory came late in the spring with the Great Train Ride, an event that changed his nickname. Yarber and three friends were hanging around Waters' Grocery one Tuesday afternoon smoking and telling lies, mostly about girls. Yarber mentioned one of the latter who lived out near John Sevier rail yards and who would, well … you know. No one believed him, but it was a particularly moldy day and it was spring, and they wanted to believe him.

The problem was that Lester wasn't around and he was the only one who had a car. Then Yarber noticed a freight train sitting at the Cherry Street crossing, only a couple hundred yards away. After a brief argument and several dares and double dares, the four of them were sitting in an empty boxcar and the train was headed for John Sevier, Southern Railway's main Knoxville switching yards.

No one paid much attention as the train picked up speed, though they were only a couple of miles from the yards. But they did pay attention when the train sped through at 60 miles per hour.

The freight's next stop was at 6:50 a.m. the next morning in Silva, N.C., in the Smoky Mountains about 150 miles southeast of Knoxville. By stopping time Yarber was answering to several nicknames, none of them flattering.

They clambered down in the Silva yards, and the other three, after asking directions, started trying to hitch a ride back to Knoxville. Yarber was left to fend for himself.

The three reluctant travelers arrived at school just as the last classes were letting out and were quick to spread the tale of their odyssey. Yarber, when he finally showed up, told a different tale. But from then on he was known as Boxcar.

*James Noel Smith captures
Yarber earning his new nickname*

Mistaken for Sam Young

Early one summer evening in the late 1970s, I was standing on a street corner just south of downtown Louisville, on the edge of the Spalding College campus, waiting for a friend. She and I were headed to a jazz workshop led by Stan Kenton and several of his band members.

The corner had the reputation – bestowed by law enforcement – of being a "24-hour intersection." There was activity there, much of it involving illegal substances, at all hours.

I was soon mistaken for someone named Sam Young, a character familiar to the neighborhood. The encounter began when I heard voices coming from a large tangle of bushes across the street. The foliage was, apparently, the refuge of a couple of men and they were arguing. The discussion had nothing to do with the academic setting – the conversation was dominated by profanity, each declaration carrying a threat of physical mayhem.

After insults were swapped for a couple of minutes, one of the men rolled out of the bushes and unsteadily got to his feet, still yelling at his buddy. Then he saw me across the street – and brightened.

Turning back toward the bush, he yelled "There's Sam Young over there and he's gonna come over here and whip your ass."

Then he motioned for me to cross the street. "Come on and take care of this idiot, Sam. He's so damned drunk he can't even stand up."

I stayed where I was. So the questioner decided to come to me. Gingerly – half walking and half sliding – he made his way to the sidewalk. About halfway across the street – ignoring oncoming traffic – he realized that I was not Sam Young. But he took it well, deciding that I was a new-found friend.

"You're not Sam," he said, sticking out his paw for a handshake. "You know him? He's a real tush hog."

"I haven't had the pleasure," I said. "But if I run into him, I'll tell him you need his help."

"You holdin'?" he then asked, hoping I had a bottle of booze.

I shook my head and, fortunately, saw my companion coming up the street. As she and I ducked into the Spalding classroom building, the drunk began trying to cross the street, cussing as he returned to his buddy in the bushes.

And Sam Young? I never did meet him, though I'm sure he was familiar to the cops covering that beat.

Big Red, Who Went to Minnesota and Died

In the late 1960s, I met a fellow University of Tennessee student who was an animal-husbandry major, specializing in beef cattle. He was a bit of a character, fancying himself a rancher. He was partial to cowboy boots and a 10-gallon hat and claimed to be an expert horseman.

His cowboy getup, he assured me, was not just a necessity in the barnyard – women found it attractive.

He also claimed expert knowledge of shorthorn cattle. And, I soon learned, the last assertion was not bull.

During Knoxville's late-summer fair, he talked me into going out to the livestock barns at Chilhowee Park, where he had a bull entered in competition. When we got to the stall housing his entry, he proudly pointed out the blue ribbon with his name on it.

Then, as we walked around the pens, he spotted someone he knew. "Come on," he said, "there's another prize-winner you need to meet." Soon, he was in the clutches of a tall female with a gorgeous head of red hair. "This is Big Red," he said with a smattering of pride.

Big Red, it turned out, was also an animal-husbandry major, and she, too, knew her way around beef cattle. Plus (and more importantly to us at the time), she knew how to get a cooler full of beer into the fairgrounds. Soon, we were sitting on bales of hay in the back of her livestock trailer having a cold brew as the two of them caught up.

Later, as my friend and I made our way back to our favorite off-campus hangout, he told me all about Big Red, how the pair of them had enjoyed a torrid fling several months earlier until he had ditched her.

It was obvious that he regretted the break-up and that he would like to re-kindle the relationship.

"Women like that – good-looking, interesting, and knowledgeable about cattle – are hard to come by," he allowed.

I could only agree.

The next time I saw my friend, he was returning from a date with Big Red. "Yep," he said. "Going great, me and her. I don't know why I let her get away."

"You told me the break-up was your idea," I reminded him.
"Well, technically that's true," he admitted. I pushed him on the reason they had split, but he hemmed and hawed. Most I could get out of him was it had to do with a barroom argument over a shorthorn-breeding arrangement.

I didn't see him for a while, so I assumed things were going well at the ranch.

Then he showed up at my door one night, drunk.

"It's over with Big Red," he said. "She sold her stock and left town. No forwarding address. I can't find out where she went."

I managed, with difficulty, to get him home. But a couple of weeks later, he was back at my door.

"I still can't find Big Red," he said. "I've been to all her hangouts: Bill's Barn, Brownie's, the Yardarm, all the Ag campus spots. No one seems to know what happened to her. I even went over to the apartment of her ex-boyfriend. He hadn't seen her, either."

The next time I saw him, I asked after Big Red. He gave me a long look.

"She went to Minnesota and died," he finally said. His demeanor told me he wasn't kidding.

Finally, he explained, he had run into one of her best friends, and she had given him the bad news. I pushed him for details, but he said that was all he had been told.

"Mysterious," he said. "Happened suddenly. I called her sister in Minnesota and she said that the doctors couldn't figure out what she was sick from, and then she just died."

Another month went by before I saw him again. "Remember Big Red?" he asked. Sure, I said. "Well, she did go to Minnesota, but she's alive and well."

What about the rumor of her death, I wanted to know.

"She spread that story so I wouldn't bother her," he said. Is it going to work, I asked?

"I think so – I told you she was smart, way too smart for me."

Uluru and the Red Men

In 1981, I spent two weeks in Australia on a travel-writing junket. Uluru – then known as Ayers Rock – was one of our stops. The published account of that trip is part of the **Wandering** section, and contains the basics of the following story, but the ending here is a mischief using aspects of aboriginal culture.

The spider was light brown in color and not tarantula-hairy – but it was larger than my hand and was clinging to the wall above my bed and I was in a place foreign to me. So I carefully exited the bed and hurried to the hotel office/bar/poolroom for information.

I was with a group of five travel writers at Ayers Rock in the middle of Australia's outback, just arrived at our hotel after a flight from Alice Springs. Our rudimentary lodging consisted of a collection of pre-fab single-story buildings that had been trucked in and assembled around a small swimming pool. It would be several years before Australia restored the rock's aboriginal name, Uluru, and a first-class resort was constructed.

Jacky proved to be a font of aboriginal knowledge, laughed

at our account of the bar in Alice, and offered tips about climbing the rock. And, when the one obnoxious member of our group made an appearance, Jacky quickly sized him up – and ignored his arrogant comments.

A Californian, he had already angered the rest of us by trying to seduce the two women traveling with us as well as every other female we encountered. After one drink of his beer, he asked the bartender about the blonde in the black bikini sunning beside the pool.

"The Doc, mate," Jacky said. "She's an anthropologist from Melbourne. Knows everything about the abo culture."

"She's not very friendly," Obnoxious answered. "Wouldn't let me take her picture."

Jacky chuckled. Then, to change the subject, "I wouldn't bother with the Doc, mate. She's way too clever for our lot."

After Obnoxious departed, and Jacky and I had each downed a couple more Foster's, the conversation returned to the Doc in the bikini.

"Earlier in the summer," he said, "there was this regular – a sawed-off jackeroo in from the bush – decided she was too uppity and tried to get physical with her beside the pool. When I noticed what was up she was kneeling over him with one knee on his chest. I encouraged the jackeroo to get back to his cows." Then he reached under the bar and brought out a book. "The Doc's latest work," he said, "all about the Red Men."

The Red Men?

"Sort of tribal police for the Anangu. Bloke does something he shouldn't, depending on what it is, might get speared in the thigh by one of the Red Men. So you see an abo with a couple of scars on his thigh, you know he's trouble. Get one in here occasionally. But you won't see anyone with more than two scars. According to the Doc, the Red Men put a death spell on the blokes who don't learn after a couple of spearings.

"In the book, she tells how it works. The bloke is forced to drink a mixture. When he passes out, the Red Man kneels with one knee on his rib cage. Enough pressure is applied to break a rib or two, forcing the bone into his lung. He wakes up, a bit sore in his chest but still able to go about his business. But over days and weeks, he gets weaker and weaker until he finally dies because of the punctured lung. And everyone in the tribe is sure it was the death spell."

So if the jackeroo doesn't return you'll know why the anthropologist was kneeling with one knee on his chest, I guessed.

"Well, mate, I haven't seen the bloke since I ran him off and that was a couple of months ago."

Melon Lust

When I returned to Knoxville to live in 1995 after a 23-year absence, a particular downtown sculpture caught my interest. The result is the column below, written for the alternative weekly, *Metropulse*. I proposed that the sculpture is meant to be of Gene Harrogate, a fictional character in "Suttree," the 1950s novel by the late Cormac McCarthy. Harrogate's debut in the book comes when a farmer catches him having sex with his watermelons. The column's basic assumption is that readers will be familiar with Harrogate and his carnal predilection:

The most striking change I noticed in my hometown was the different downtown landscape. The people were fewer in number and the activity was closer to the river, around the intersection of Main and Gay where only the old courthouse and the Andrew Johnson Hotel remained from my day.

The banking Butcher Brothers, Jake and C.H., had erected ostentatious phallic towers on either side of Main, their mirrored-glass walls gleaming like pinkie diamonds. In the process they had taken out a parking lot and the Gateway Book Store, one of my favorite hangouts.

The northwest corner was dominated by the more refined "campus" constructed by Knoxville's other smooth-talker of national renown, Chris Whittle, which in its stated homage to the architecture of Thomas Jefferson, is even more pretentious than the Butcher baubles. Whittle's building had replaced the Trailways Bus Station and, thanks to city generosity, a block of Market Street.

A block north at Church and Gay was another new office building, called, in developer dialect, Two Centre Square. Anchored by a bank, it had replaced an open-all-night Krystal and two perfectly good upstairs pool halls, one doubling as a bookie joint.

Across the street had been Blaufeld's, where Henry Nichols once served up the city's best chili dog and Kenneth Shelton served up a particularly skewed viewpoint of the local scene. Blaufeld's was long gone.

The Two Centre Square builders, using red brick, did manage to create an edifice more graceful than the Butchers' monuments. And, in setting their building back from the corner, they had left room for the sculpture of a rower in his boat. Of all the changes, I found this statue the most puzzling.

Is this waterless river rat sinking or rising from the brick? And who does he represent?

He's relatively modern, as his raiment includes a baseball cap, so he's not supposed to be Admiral David Farragut, Knox County native and Civil War hero.

I asked cohorts from my earlier time here, knowledgeable Knoxvillians who hadn't strayed as I had.

Jim Dykes, fisherman and retired author of a *Journal* column called "Without a Paddle," suggested it was a stylized likeness of himself.

But, I pointed out, instead of being without a paddle, the boat's occupant is equipped with two oars. "And you never wear a baseball cap," I said.

"Artistic license," Dykes answered, unconvincingly.

Someone else – it may have been adman/producer Tom Jester – thought it a composite of Knoxville's more famous hustlers, struggling to keep their schemes afloat: William Blount, Jake and C.H. Butcher, Chris Whittle.
But again, the rower's clothing suggests otherwise. He's not in 18th century garb, or a banker's suit, or a cape.

Another suggested the *Journal's* long-time sports columnist, the late Tom Anderson, who frequently wrote about his johnboat, the Dodd Dam.

But Anderson, despised by the city's establishment as he was, isn't a likely candidate for such honor. Anderson, in fact, holds the distinction of being the only Knoxville sportswriter to be permanently banned from University of Tennessee facilities. Couldn't be him.

I looked at other non-historic possibilities. Not business – Knoxville never had a fishing industry. Not sports – he doesn't look like Bob Suffridge or Big John Tate or Peyton Manning. Literary? George Washington Harris' Sut Lovingood? Possible, though there's that baseball cap.

But Sut Lovingood leads to another fictitious Sut, a more modern one. Cormac McCarthy's Suttree was set in the 1950s. And one of that novel's most memorable characters, Gene Harrogate, certainly deserves to be bronzed.

Harrogate is the hustling "country mouse" to Suttree's "city mouse." When he isn't residing at the sheriff department's workhouse, Harrogate lives on the Tennessee River or under the viaduct across First Creek. Though he uses the hood of a car for his boat and he catches bats instead of fish, during one period he does try to make his living from the river. And a later scheme involves tunneling underground to reach the city's bank vaults. He could be attempting to row out of the bank's basement.
The likeness has to be of Gene Harrogate.

And that conclusion lends itself to a proposal for the city fathers, a way we can not only honor one of Knoxville's most talented writers and his innovative creation, but also put some life into downtown during the summer.

The Annual Gene Harrogate Watermelon Festival could take place in the dead days between the end of spring's Dogwood Arts Festival and the start of UT football season.

Harrogate's love of watermelon is indelibly documented by McCarthy, and the boat sculpture is naturally shaped for filling with ice and watermelons.

The festivities could start with an actual rowboat race on the river. Prizes could be awarded to the person bringing in the most bats and to the person concocting the most outlandish money-making scheme (Blounts, Butchers, and Whittles not eligible). The mayor could read aloud Harrogate's introduction in Suttree.

And then everyone could gather around for a luscious piece of watermelon.

Grits in Laramie, Wyoming

On the way to Elko, Nevada, in late January 2018 to cover the 35th Annual Cowboy Poetry Gathering for *The New York Times*, I stopped in a café outside Laramie for breakfast. A surprising menu and a charming waitress led to this fictionalized account (only the "skijoring" part is fiction, though the sport does exist in Scandinavia):

As the rising sun was making its move to the east, I spotted an open cafe at the Laramie exit of Interstate 80. I had gotten out of Denver, 75 miles south, an hour or so earlier while it was still dark. It was the last week in January and I was on my way to Elko, Nevada. Luckily, I had not been hampered by snow — yet.

The Chuckwagon was lit up and serving breakfast. Inside, I found a table, and a lissome blonde waitress whose name tag said she went by Cheyenne. She took my order for hot tea while I checked the menu. The usual breakfast dishes were featured, but two entries caught my attention. Eggs Benedict could be had with avocado and a side for $6.99. And one of the side options was grits.

Now, I've had grits all over the South — from watery and inedible to luxuriously silky and delectable. But grits in Wyoming? At a place called The Chuckwagon? Asked if the grits' maker was from the South, Cheyenne answered that the kitchen was staffed by a husband and wife from Costa Rica. "So, yep, way south."

Had she tried them? She laughed, "I'm just an 18-year-old cowgirl. I've never been south of Denver, so what would I know?" She added emphasis to her smile with a wink.

"And the joke's on me," I said, ordering a side of grits – just out of curiosity – to go with Eggs Benedict, fried potatos and Costa Rican salsa.

Now, Cheyenne may have been only 18 and a Wyoming cowgirl, but she had a winning way that was just what an old man needed early on a chilly January morning, especially if he was headed into a snowstorm just east of Salt Lake City. Add her playfulness, the long legs and bright blue eyes, and, well, she had skillfully hooked me for a generous tip.

These grits are terrible, I told her. "No charge," she said. Then, as I got up to go, she added, "You're not leaving already, are you?"

"Cheyenne, I would love to stay — and maybe teach your cook to make grits," I said, "but I've got to beat the weather to Salt Lake and then make Elko the next day."

She rung me up, then, with another wink, handed me a home-baked cookie "to make up for the grits."

So a week later, head full of cowpoke couplets, I was on my way east on Interstate 80 right about daybreak when I noticed that Laramie was the next exit — and realized that The Chuckwagon was sure to be open. When I walked in, Cheyenne welcomed me back, seated me and brought a hot tea without my asking. "Eggs Benedict," I said, with potatos and salsa. "No grits this time?" she said, knowing the answer. When she returned with more hot water for my tea, I noticed her belt buckle was one of those big, blingy things that usually mean a triumphant rodeo turn.

"What did you win that for?" I asked.

"Barrel-racing," she said with a hint of pride.

Eggs delivered and consumed, along with more hot tea, I started to get up and head out.

"What's your hurry?" Cheyenne asked.

"I've got to get to Denver and then cross Kansas ahead of the weather."

"Where you going?" she wanted to know.

"Knoxville, Tennessee, in the Smoky Mountains," I answered.

"You came all the way out here, in the winter, just to do a story on a bunch of cowboys?" Yep, I said. "And I'd do it again — it was a great time. Of course, I was lucky with the weather, knock on wood because I'm not home yet."

"Supposed to snow here tomorrow," she said.

"So what do Laramie folks do for fun during the winter?" I asked. "Don't barrel-race in the snow, do you?"

"Skijoring," she answered.

"What?" I wanted to know.

"Skijoring — we ski while being pulled by horses. There are

races, and it can get plenty rough." She delivered that last line with a coy look that let me know she could handle it.

"You won any belt buckles for that?"

"Not yet, but there's a big meet in a couple of weeks and I'm entered. You ought to hang around and write a story about me."

I smiled. "Cheyenne, much as I would like to stay and watch you skijor, unfortunately I've got deadlines to meet and the entire state of Kansas to cross."

So, with Cheyenne's "drive carefully" ringing in my ears and a couple of fresh-baked cookies in hand, I hit the road, staying just ahead of bad weather all the way home to Knoxville, accompanied by the memory of a saucy-sweet cowgirl.

Christmas stories

In 1981 when I was working at *The Dallas Times Herald*, we decided to include a couple of Christmas memories in our late-December issue of *Westward*. My contribution was a fictional goof that I had dreamed up a couple of years earlier but had never written. The story also appeared in the Sunday magazines published by *The Philadelphia Inquirer* and *The Detroit Free Press*.

Several years later I posted it on Facebook during the holidays, and there was enough of a positive response that I began featuring a Christmas-themed goof every year. Below are a half dozen, two of them involving holiday tales related by friends. The photo of me as a Texas-themed Santa was taken by the *Times Herald's* Michael S. Wirtz

The Gift

Since we'll be in the new house in the country soon, we loaded up the SUV and drove out there last weekend to see how things were going. There was a nip in the air, so I wore the cardigan sweater I got for Christmas a couple of years ago. During the drive, The Wife reminded me that if it wasn't for the cardigan, we wouldn't be moving at all. Though I detected a note of smugness in her voice, I let it pass.

I would never have bought a cardigan for myself. It was a gift, of course. Even after I received it, I didn't intend to wear it. After making the obligatory to-do over it in front of the giver, I placed it on the shelf of my closet, hoping it would be forgotten. But the giver kept asking about it, and guilt being unrelenting, I started wearing it to insure household peace.

Understand, I have nothing against cardigans. They're generally attractive and they're functional. The problem with cardigans is that they imply so much about you. And though the implication is quiet, it's inescapable.

For example, a cardigan wearer is expected to smoke a pipe. Those little pockets on the side were designed to hold a pipe and tobacco. What other possible use could they have? They're too small for your hands.

I have always considered pipe smokers as pompous asses, fouling the air with their aromatic and all-too-English tobacco mixes. Every pipe smoker I've known practices the kind of fatuous snobbery that reaches its pinnacle with Harris tweeds and Wellingtons. I have always treated pipe smokers with disdain, if not outright hostility.

I bought the pipe one Saturday morning when I had to run down to the hardware store to pick up some flanges (I was wearing the cardigan) and it was there beside the cash register, nestled in a velvet-lined box and packaged with a tin of Special Tartan Blend tobacco.

Soon the cardigan became a fixture, and I kept getting comments about how "English" or how "dashing" I looked. So I bought one of those herringbone-wool caps that you see in old automobile advertisements. You know, the car is stuck in the mud of a country lane, and the bonneted lady is exasperated and her date is perplexed (but still dashing) as he tries to figure out how to unstick the car. Of course, his cap matches his knickers. The Wife couldn't find a pair of herringbone-wool knickers, so we settled for corduroy.

The first thoughts about the townhouse being too small, and too — well, modern — came when I was sitting at the kitchen island, thumbing through an Orvis catalog. I was wearing my cardigan and smoking a pipeful of the tobacco that I have specially blended down at the Briar and Bowl. It was a blustery day, and I was appreciating the coziness of my situation when The Wife came in and remarked about how nice it would be to have an old-fashioned stone fireplace. She added that with my pipe and cardigan, I would look really nice in front of a roaring blaze.

The next day we drove out into the country, tooling around the backwoods in the BMW, breathing healthy autumn air, watching the smoke curl from the stone chimneys of picture-perfect farmhouses scattered among the woods and fields.

We watched a man saddle his horse, dog sitting dutifully by his side. We stopped in a country store and bought apples and talked with the tanned and cheerful postmistress of a crossroad named Spillcorn or Cornpone or something similarly bucolic. On the way back we talked about the advantages of Life in the Country.

The Lab came a little later, when a friend — I think it was LaFong — remarked that all I needed to complete the picture was one of those black dogs that are born with limp ducks in their mouths. A few days later I brought home the pup and we named it Harris. Full of puppy energy, Harris likes to bound around the patio, chasing the pigeons that try to land on the railing. It is sort of sad, knowing that he would rather be splashing through some icy bog on the mission for which his breed was bred — to bring back the dead waterfowl his master has just brought down with a single blast of his shotgun.

As Harris has grown he has begun to create problems in the condo. Anytime there is more than two guests, he has to be shut out on the patio. There just isn't room. He sits and peers inside, sad-eyed. "He's so lonely," The Wife points out.

So we bought him a playmate, another Lab, which we named Plaid. Plaid quickly caught on to the pigeon game, and there are a lot of great times watching the two of them playing. They also do some damage, knocking over the glass block and its gladiolas. We've had to give up on the fresh flowers.

Eventually, we made more trips to the country, so the dogs could get out and run, and discovered that the Beemer just wasn't big enough for us and the dogs. Especially when we crammed in the bushel of apples and the roasting ears and the pole beans. We decided on the Lexus SUV in a sort of chocolate brown, a restful earth color.

On our fourth trip out we found the land — 10 acres, about half of it wooded with a pond at the edge of the trees. The Wife pointed out that the small rise with the fieldstone outcroppings on the slope would be a perfect homesite.

And to the rear, running into the woods, are the remains of an old stone fence. We're using some of the stone for the fireplace. It works well with the look the builder is giving the place.

Last trip out I cut a cord or so of firewood from a red oak that had fallen in the woods and stacked it next to the remains of the fence. We'll need it when it gets colder and there is snow on the ground.

The Wife had taken the Lexus and was making the rounds of the antique stores, looking for primitives to furnish the house. (We've promised all the modern, high-tech stuff to LaFong.) When she returned, I was helping her unload her purchase, a late-19th-century pie safe, when she noticed a hole in the elbow of the cardigan.

"Maybe you'll get a new one for Christmas," she predicted, with a knowing smile.

Over the Highway & Through the Fields

A couple of days after Christmas a few years back I got a phone call from a Boston friend. His first words were "I just had a Flannery O'Connor experience."

Now, my friend is a true Bostonian – born in Boston, went to college in Boston, journalism career in Boston. But he had recently married a woman from eastern North Carolina, and he had spent the Christmas holidays with her family, way south of his geographical comfort zone.

Being a journalist, my friend usually is not fazed by new experiences, but too much of his knowledge of the South was based on conversations with me and other newspaper veterans from south of the Mason-Dixon. And we Southerners are known to exaggerate when talking about our background, and, perhaps more damning, to nurture eccentricity in fellow Southerners to ensure we have dependable sources for our tales.

I wanted details, and he quickly obliged. The day after Christmas, it seems, featured copious amounts of bourbon, runaway ice, a great-uncle who had lost his driver's license because of DUI incidents, and moonshine. "Instead of Over the River and Through the Woods," he said, "it was Over the Highway and Through the Fields."

Early on the 26th, one of his bride's uncles, who we'll call Doc, made the decision to visit HIS brother, who lived a few miles away. "Turned out that the brothers are both particularly eccentric," my friend said. "Because of the loss of his license, Doc could not risk driving on the highway, so the route was through the fields to the highway, where he carefully looked in both directions for any sign of the law, then gunned his car across the road before continuing on through more fields to the brother's place, a rambling old farmhouse.

"Parked in the yard was one of those Chevrolet Impalas from the '70s, you know, about the size of Indiana; there was a For Sale sign posted inside the windshield.

"After a moonshine-fueled welcome, the bourbon came out, and we were introduced to the brother's new refrigerator, which featured an ice-maker with the dispenser in the door. The bourbon required ice, of course, but the brothers had not mastered the dispenser and ice was soon flying all over the kitchen. It was like ice-skating on linoleum.

"When I went to the bathroom, there were four stand-up urinals. I guess they were from an old theater or some public building and they had gotten a deal on 'em. They were all connected to the plumbing; apparently the thinking was, if you're going to plumb one, might as well plumb them all.

"The bourbon kept flowing, and the flying ice was making

it more difficult to maneuver, so I started trying to regulate my intake by taking small sips. That turned out to be the best decision, as it was eventually decided that I should see the beaver dam down on the other side of the farm, and since I possessed a valid driver's license I was drafted to be the wheelman.

"The for-sale sign was removed from the Chevy and we set off across the fields. The Chevy apparently still had its original shocks and the fields had exacted a heavy toll. Controlling the Impala was like handling a winter sled in New England. The tires were baloney skins and a lot of quick spinning of the steering wheel was the only way to keep the car from bogging down in mud.

"Sure, there was a beaver dam on the creek. It had flooded maybe a low acre, and the adjacent saplings had suffered the beavers' craftsmanship. Not a beaver in sight. So, for all the build-up and transportation perils what we had was essentially a visit to an irrigation pond.

"As I started the drive back to the farmhouse, I worried I would never gain traction. And I was NOT walking back through those barren, furrowed acres with a pair of drunk Tarheels, who seemed unconcerned – or oblivious – to any potential predicament.

"A successful return trip, I suppose, was all that kept my motoring skills from being the most memorable aspect of the outing. Funny what passes for holiday entertainment in Dorches, North Carolina."

Christmas Parade

My experience with Christmas parades was limited to attending several when I was a child. But a couple of my East High School buddies had starring roles in Knoxville's 1962 Christmas parade. I was reminded of their participation in 2013 at our 50th high school reunion.

David Evans and I had laughed earlier over the story he told of how he and Mike Lawson were suspended for the entire first week after school re-opened following the Christmas holiday.

Evans and Lawson were serious gearheads and, though I only had occasional access to my dad's Ford station wagon, I always gravitated to them when they wheeled into the school parking lot with something that was noisier and sometimes much more powerful than anything else in sight. Plus, Evans was a prankster, a valued attribute in high school.

Lawson, sadly, had passed away a couple of years earlier, but Evans was coaxed to the microphone at the reunion to tell the story. Lawson, he said, would want full credit. "Mike's contribution, a new Chevy with a 409 engine and a Hurst four-speed, was essential to our being in the parade," he explained.

When the pair noticed the date and time for the event, they decided they should grace the festivities. Lawson then convinced his older brother to loan him his Chevy. "We told him that we would make his car the star of the parade, second only to Santa himself," Evans told us.

As the parade assembly started a couple of blocks from

downtown early on the designated morning, the pair eased up to the crowd, Lawson in the Chevy, Evans in his similarly equipped hot rod, both cars newly cleaned and waxed. "We waited until all the bands and floats had been lined up, Santa in his place of honor," Evans said, "and then we joined the back of the line." The music started and the parade slowly made its way downtown.

"We followed closely for the first block or two, then we slowed way down until we were several car lengths back. We then popped clutches and burned rubber, tires screaming, till we had caught up.

"Naturally, that got the attention of the crowd – and of the two cops slowly marching alongside the last band. They quickly routed us away from the rest of the parade, and we got tickets for reckless driving." And how did Buford Bible, the school principal, find out?

"Well," Evans explained, "we wanted to give the automotive repair classes proper credit, so we made banners that said East High School and put them on the cars. But Mr. Bible didn't agree when I argued that we just wanted to make our school proud."

James Noel Smith's version of an angry Santa

Sadly, Evans died a couple of months after the reunion.

Lori & Christmas in Miami

The Five Dames was a classic New York delicatessen – an extensive selection of well-prepared hot meals ranging from split-pea soup to knish as well as sandwiches piled with corned beef or home-made chopped chicken liver. But the Five Dames was in Miami – actually only barely in Miami. It was on the southwest edge, closer to Homestead and the Everglades than to Miami proper. And, because it was an easy walk from the apartment Larry Hobbs and I shared off Kendall Drive, we were frequent customers.

I was a copy editor at *The Miami Herald* and Hobbs, a Knoxville friend, was working for The Associated Press. About the same time I was offered a job at *The Herald* in late 1972 he was transferred to Miami, so we got an apartment together. Our work space in Herald Plaza was downtown, overlooking Biscayne Bay, but we had ended up at a new complex 25 or so miles away called Cherry Grove – balconies, a fancy night-lit swimming pool and the also-new strip mall next door that housed the Five Dames.

The deli was owned by a couple of brothers, one of them named Herb, and he honored his daughters by tagging the place for them. All the girls seemed to be working there, though I'm sure it was only the oldest pair, the younger ones drifting in and out. Herb ran the register; his brother manned the deli counter.

As Hobbs and I were approaching our first palm-tree Christmas we got a call from another Knoxville friend. Lori had grown up in Saudi Arabia; her dad worked for Aramco, the oil conglomerate. She was attending the University of Tennessee and did not have the money – or the desire – to return to the Mideast for the holidays. Did we want a guest? We told her she was more than welcome and were soon picking her up at Miami International Airport.

Because we were in the news business Hobbs and I would be working through the holidays, and that meant that Lori was going to be stuck at Cherry Grove without a vehicle. So on her first day in south Florida I introduced her to the Five Dames at lunch time before I headed to work. Hobbs was already gone.

As I was settling up with Herb, Lori decided deli fare was in order since she was going to be hanging around the pool and didn't want to have to prepare something hot for dinner. She was checking out the selection when Herb's brother prodded her to hurry up.

Now, Lori had the impish appeal you would expect of a 20-year-old college girl. But the time she had spent in Beirut and Bahrain meant that she was much more world-wise than most 20-year-olds. She looked up and, loud enough to be heard throughout the restaurant, said "Don't give me any of your f------ New York b-------." When Herb looked at me I started laughing, then he did too. The daughter who was present joined us, and, finally, the deli-counter brother couldn't help but laugh himself.

A week later, when it was time for Lori to return to Knoxville, she insisted on a last visit to Five Dames to say good-bye to her new friends.

Christmas Sweaters

Holidays are times of tradition – friends and family crowding around the Christmas tree, gifts carefully chosen and beautifully presented, news of far-flung family members related.

Then there are the turkeys – both the birds that are lovingly stuffed and roasted and the relatives who merit that nickname because of boorish behavior. But sometimes the traditions are carried on year to year because they provide a humorous counter to the sentimental gatherings usually associated with the holidays.

Such is the case with my friend Suggs and his wife, who he calls The Missus. Their Christmas-eve tradition includes attending services at the Episcopal church followed with a stop at the neighborhood Applebee's, where they leisurely dine at a table in the bar. The attraction is not the food, but the scene, which The Missus, referencing her musical background, calls The Dance of the Sugar Plum Fairies.

"The single men and women, all of a certain age – here a trio of women, there a foursome of men – check the room for potential partners," Suggs explains. "A male will spot a woman he thinks might be interesting. He may be attracted because of her Christmas sweater, or because of her discreetly pitched giggle, or because of her embarrassment at her friend's loud laughter. He will then offer to buy her a drink.

"He might then be invited to join her and her friends. Maybe two tables are pulled together and a small party commences. There might be a comparison of holiday sweaters, with ensuing laughter."

Of course all is not always merry, he adds.

"Sometimes the female will arise to visit the bathroom. The male will then wait and wait and wait. Eventually, realizing that she has probably slipped away without his noticing, he will start over, looking around the room for another likely candidate."

The tradition began for Suggs and The Missus a dozen years ago. "At first," he says, "The Missus started noticing the sweaters, making fun of the various designs. Then we would decide on which sweaters would make the funniest pairings – maybe a Beavis and Butthead with a cuddly Paddington bear, or a Grinch with a decked-out dachshund.

"A couple of years ago there was a would-be player wearing a red-nosed reindeer sweater whose own nose was brighter than the depiction on his outfit. But he had the last laugh – he left Applebee's with the woman who was his first choice. Her sweater was a simple number, red and green with white snowflakes.

"I guess," the Missus adds, "that sometimes the Dance of the Sugar Plum Fairies can produce magic no matter what the venue."

Frosty & His Sibling

Sometime in the mid-1960s, a pregnant cat was dropped off alongside the field that bordered my parents' house in east Knox County. Soon, the mother and four kittens showed up at Mom's back door. Naturally, they were fed, but attempts to corral them were mostly futile.

Momma Cat and three of the kittens avoided capture, but one, a white male whose long hair gave him a regal appearance, decided that as long as the food was tasty, he could put up with semi-confinement. By Christmas time, my mother had named him Frosty, after the snowman of holiday fame.

Frosty soon had the run of the house. And he took advantage of it. In keeping with my mother's propensity for pranks,

Frosty soon developed one of his own – at her expense. When Frosty would emerge from his preferred hiding place and had determined that Mom was at the kitchen stove, he would sprint down the hall, jump to one of the dining-room chairs and leap through the opening over the range onto my mother.

The first time he pulled this trick, disaster was averted only because Mom had not yet filled the pot she was holding. As the pot clanged across the floor Frosty quickly disappeared back down the hall.

But he apparently liked the game and it soon became common. Disasters were avoided only because of the thumping noises caused by Frosty's running leaps across the dining room. The thumps alerted Mom to what was coming and she would duck out of the way and Frosty would fly through the opening and then slide across the kitchen linoleum.

My brother Ben, who was still living at home, witnessed one of the episodes and, relishing the fact that Frosty's fun was at Mom's expense, started telling visitors from the neighborhood about the prankster nature – and the athleticism – of her cat.

Ben and Frosty

They were skeptical until Lucy Stott, who lived down the street, was startled by a leaping white blur one day while she was having coffee at our dining-room table. Mom claimed that Lucy's scream was so loud that Mrs. O'Neal, who lived several houses away, called to see if everything was OK.

Ben soon became Frosty's favorite Wohlwend. I suspect that he encouraged Frosty by taking up our mother's position at the stove and rattling a pan or two to get his attention. After catching him when he leaped, Ben would then give him his favorite reward.

Frosty didn't go for the usual treats – he liked plain, soft white bread. Loaves of Sunbeam were kept in a kitchen drawer near the floor, so he would sit there until someone gave him a slice. (He also developed a taste for skillet-made cornbread – we quickly learned to keep any leftovers in the oven so he could not help himself).

At about age 7, Frosty disappeared. Ben found his body in the back yard – we decided he was a victim of distemper. Later, other cats and dogs became part of the household but none could match Frosty.

One of Frosty's siblings, another male, left our neighborhood one autumn day via unusual circumstances. We never corralled him and he didn't have a name, so I'll call him Sib. A tabby with yellowish hair, Sib got around, judging by the appearance of the offspring of other strays in the neighborhood. Some kittens sported Frosty's long-haired looks, others Sib's mackerel-tabby coat.

My dad drove a Ford F100 pick-up truck to and from his job at the Alcoa plant in adjoining Blount County. His one-way commute was a good 35 miles. The trip was primarily by interstate highway and Dad had the timing worked out so that he could make it to work without stopping: Rutledge Pike (US 11W) to Interstate 40, exit Alcoa Highway (US 129), across the Tennessee River bridge then a long run parallel to the water until he crossed the Stock Creek embayment, then past the Lakeview Drive-in and the fortune-teller's house. Then, just shy of the airport, he would make two left-hand turns into the parking lot of Alcoa's North Plant.

One day, as he rolled to a stop, he noticed an orange streak high-tailing for the adjoining woods. Dad quickly realized it was Sib, who had accompanied him from our house in Spring Place subdivision. We all knew that Sib liked to sleep in the truck's engine bay, where it was warm and relatively safe from neighborhood dogs. On that particular day, he apparently was sleeping soundly, not waking until the truck was underway – he was smart enough not to jump until the truck had stopped.

Dad checked under the hood before he departed work eight hours later, but there was no sign of Sib. So we assumed that he would now be making his night-time rounds in the neighborhoods around the sprawling Alcoa facility.

Forgotten Episodes in Southern History

Late one night in 1988, Stanley Booth and I were leaving a blues club in Atlanta after a show by Sleepy LaBeef when he mentioned James Brown, the subject of a story he was working on for Esquire magazine. I don't remember the context, and I have no idea of the origination of my next comment:

"You know it's too bad that James Brown never toured with Flannery O'Connor."

The absurdity was evident, and Stanley and I laughed until we had exhausted the subject, realizing that anything we tried to add would only weaken the elemental looniness.

A couple of weeks later I was involved in a telephone conversation with Jim Morgan, the editorial director of Southern magazine, a then-new publication based in Little Rock. As an afterthought, I told him about the imagined James Brown/Flannery O'Connor tour.

After we laughed, he suggested I try to figure out a way to use the idea for a humor feature. A couple of weeks later, after a collaborative phone conversation with illustrator James Noel Smith, I was again talking to Morgan, this time pitching a concrete idea. Southern published the result in April 1988.

Citing "audience confusion" the promoter cancels the remaining dates of the 1962 James Brown - Flannery O'Connor Tour after the first show in Florence, South Carolina.

George Corley Wallace withdraws from his first Presidential attempt after an unscrupulous political opponent reveals that the Alabama governor has never actually seen Rock City.

Members of North Carolina's Lost Colony are discovered selling chenille bedspreads at the South's first roadside attraction, near present-day Jellico, Tennessee.

At Speed

Fast cars, including driving 120 miles per hour behind the wheel of a Jaguar in South Florida. And racetime visits to Road Atlanta, Sebring, Daytona, Watkins Glen, Indianapolis and LeMans, France. Featuring champagne with Dick Smothers, crashing the Datsun Awards Banquet in Atlanta, and sharing space with the Hawaiian Tropic girls and Paul Newman on the starting grid at the 24 Heures du Mans.

Along about 1959, when I was 14, I graduated from my 1958 Chevrolet to my dad's 1953 Ford station wagon. I should point out that the Chevy was a plastic model about four inches in length that I had customized with fine-grade sandpaper. The station wagon was real, two-toned a couple of shades of brown, powered by flat-head V-8, gear-shift three-on-the-tree.

Sometimes my dad would catch a ride from our house in Burlington, the east Knoxville neighborhood where I grew up, to the Alcoa plant where he was a machinist. That usually happened when Mom needed the car for errands. And Mom would allow me to move the car back and forth in the driveway so I could practice using the clutch – understand, I could not take the car into the street, and the drive was too short to go through the gears. But I could at least practice my footwork.

My automotive hero was neighbor Earl Presley, a couple of years older, who had already obtained his driver's license. Earl's brother David had bought a used pre-war car, which inspired Earl to study the state-issued pamphlet on the rules of the road so he could pass the license test. The brothers, taking advantage of their wheels, soon were bragging about attending Saturday-night races at Ashway Speedway, a half-mile dirt oval a few miles east of where we lived. And, when I agreed to their demand for gas money, they invited me along.

Ashway participants' vehicles were primarily pre-war coupes, souped up with whatever power plants their owners could salvage. Most sported black paint, though some were still in the primer stage. All of them were noisy.

Ashway was located just off U.S. 11 East, the main highway to Newport and the North Carolina state line. Newport, the Cocke County seat, was in the foothills of the Great Smoky Mountains and notorious as a center for moonshining. Fast cars, twisting mountain roads, daredevil drivers – on Saturday nights, Ashway Speedway was a gathering place for would-be scofflaws.

The facility featured a concrete grandstand just above the start-finish line, sturdy seating for several dozen fans.

The track itself was banked, the second and third turns steep enough so that any car that went over the side was out of sight.

The area's dominant driver was a Knoxvillian who went by an incongruous nickname: Herb Estes was known to his fans as "Tootle". Later, he graduated from Ashway to greater fame racing on north-Georgia tracks, and was inducted into the dirt-track hall of fame several years after his 1982 death.

I don't recall how Tootle fared on the night when I first watched him at work – my standout memory from that night is the driver who lost control on the second turn and disappeared over the bank, halting the race. Crew members and other drivers sprinted after him as everyone waited. Finally, the driver was led over the lip of the bank and back onto the track, held up by a couple of others. Wobbling, he waved at the crowd.

The announcer proclaimed that he was OK, but the fans seated next to us, familiar with the driver, assured us that he was just drunk. "He likes his 'shine," one of them told us. "Never races sober," said another.

There were other occasional treks to Ashway, and, when I was living in Miami in the mid-1970s, a friend and I visited a course in Hialeah where the track was completely flat and the facilities were a bit more sophisticated: A chain-link fence separated the grandstand from the competitors. But the banged-up condition of the vehicles and the seemingly daredevil driving was similar to Ashway action.

After I obtained my driver's license and my dad had bought a second car for Mom's use, I was able to venture beyond our driveway. The Ford wagon was the last straight-shift car to grace our driveway – Mom insisted on an automatic transmission.

There was a succession of vehicles, all purchased used, all about five years old. Dad, adept at keeping cars in running order, had decided that the wisest approach to car ownership was to buy one that was five years old, add another five years of use, then repeat the process. Sometimes we had two Fords, sometimes it was a Ford and a Chevy. He stayed away from Chrysler products, calling them "frogs". My attempts to get an explanation of the nickname were fruitless.

But my friend Buddy Slack's mom drove a "frog." She had a pale green Chrysler station wagon, tricked out with all the luxuries of the day. And she had no idea that Slack and I were regularly drag-racing our station wagons on Magnolia Avenue, the four-lane highway that bisected Burlington.

Dad's vehicle at the time was another Ford wagon, also in brown and white two-tone livery, but with an automatic transmission. The Chrysler was equipped with a TorqueFlite automatic unit. So our take-offs were relatively sedate – no popping of clutches and burning rubber. Besides, most of the time the vehicles were weighted down with the female passengers we were trying to impress.

Though my vehicles were prosaic – Dad insisted that the most important attribute of a car was getting him to work and back – by the time I started looking for a car of my own, I was leaning toward something more exotic. The owner of the Burlington movie theater we frequented owned an English sports car, a real automobile in my eyes. He drove a pristine early-1950s Jaguar XK roadster, pearl white with red-leather interior. When he would motor through the neighborhood, top down of course, everyone noticed.

In 1966, after I was promoted to a full-time job at *The Knoxville Journal*, I was forced to buy a car. *The Journal* was the morning daily, which meant that my hours were 2 p.m. to 11 p.m., perfect for a University of Tennessee sophomore. I could schedule my classes in the mornings, then walk downtown to *The Journal*. After work, I would catch the last bus from downtown, exiting at the route turn-around about a half-mile from our house.

Unfortunately, the news business does not always function on time, and too often I would miss the last bus and my dad would have to come and get me. He soon let me know that it was time I bought a car.

I soon found a vehicle to match my particular wants – a dove-gray Mark I Jaguar sedan with automatic transmission and navy-leather interior. It was new in 1960, one of the last of the Mark I line to roll off the assembly line.

The Mark 1 Jaguar, with a white-water raft aboard

The dash featured burled walnut trim and the engine was Jag's storied duel-overhead-cam 3.4 litre, capable (if the speedometer could be believed) of 140 miles an hour.

A neighbor knew the dealer and arranged for me to borrow the car for a weekend try-out. Dad and I spent Saturday morning showing off the car at Mayford Mitchell's Esso station in Burlington. Though my dad was primarily a Ford aficionado, he appreciated the mechanics of the Jag, and was especially amazed at the tight handling. "It goes where you point it," he told Mayford.

Though the Jag's automatic transmission brought scoffs from my Burlington friends, the Jag served me well. It was fast, it impressed the girls, and it was dependable. It was also exotic enough so that most of the Burlington hot rodders had no idea what it was. Plus, when I would gas up at Mayford's, he would always get me to pop the hood so he could show the engine to the station's regulars. "Dual overhead cams," he would explain knowingly.

The car's understated looks did not scream "speed" like the Detroit products of the day, an attribute that I used to help burnish my image. Once, returning to Knoxville from a weekend with friends at East Tennessee State University in Johnson City, I was stopped at a red light in Greeneville when a new Chevy pulled up beside me. The driver nodded at me, and then took off when the light changed. He was doing 70 when I passed him, then he caught me at about 85, but I kept pulling away until I had to slow as we entered Morristown.

"What is that?" he yelled through the open window. I pulled into a station and after telling him it was a Jaguar, popped the hood so he could check out the engine. As I explained the dual-overhead-cam setup his girlfriend admired the burled-walnut dashboard. "She thought you were driving a '53 Plymouth," he said. He then showed me the engine in his Chevy, the relatively new 409 V-8.

But the Jag's glory moment came in late summer 1967 when I drove it to Miami and back. I had convinced a couple of friends, Danny Meador and Kenny Bounds, to join me on an "overseas" adventure. I had discovered that Pan American airlines would fly us from Miami to Nassau – round trip – for $28 each.

Our journey was a success but unaware of the high cost of beer in the Bahamas, we had spent most of our money. When I paid the parking fee for the Jag at Miami International Airport, I was left with less than $5. Meador and Bounds each claimed they had even less.

I wasn't worried about getting home because Dad had loaned me his gasoline credit card in case of emergency. We headed north for Daytona, knowing that our beer-drinking was at an end until we reached Knoxville. From previous Spring Break trips, we knew we could not spend the night on the beach, but we could sleep on the sand during the day, so our plan was to drive all night to reach Daytona at daybreak.

So, about 2 a.m. or so, I was driving north on U.S. 1, Danny riding shotgun and Bounds asleep in the back. Danny wondered out loud how fast we were going. "About 80," I said after a glance at the speedometer. "But it'll do more," I added. Soon, on a two-lane highway that we had to ourselves, we were doing just above 120 miles per hour. And I kept it there for about 30 miles – until Danny spotted a red light in the distance and I slowed down. This was long before Interstate 95, of course, and long before the east coast of Florida was one extended beachfront development.

Details are a bit hazy nowadays, but as I recall the light that brought us to a stop was on the outskirts of Vero Beach. And I know that we arrived at Daytona just as daylight was beginning to warm the white sand that the area is famous for. We constructed a Jaguar/tent lean-to, and, after I had evicted Bounds from the back seat so I could claim it, I was soon asleep.

I first became aware of my dad's mechanic skills when I was a child. During World War II, there was a shortage of automobiles and Dad, who as an employee of Alcoa was exempt from the military, supplemented his income by fixing cars and re-selling them.

One of my earliest memories is of a couple of sedans sitting beside our house awaiting my dad's expert efforts. As I grew older I learned to appreciate his skills and his attitude toward transportation.

But when I bought the Jaguar he was impressed by its mechanics, especially the elegant appearance of its dual-overhead-cam engine. The design, he realized, delivered its power much more efficiently than anything that Detroit had to offer. After I test-drove it from the used-car lot he did the same, voicing his approval though he wasn't sure of its dependability.

But if there were problems, I could depend on Dad to figure out a solution. Once, during a snowstorm, the ignition key broke while I was trying to penetrate the ice that had accumulated in the door handle. So Dad hot-wired it, solving the problem until I could get another key. At one point, we even removed and rebuilt the water pump, a project that took all day.

When I left Knoxville for Europe in 1972, the Jag remained at my parents' house. When I returned a couple of months later, my mom told me that Dad drove the Jag to work every day, a round trip of about 60 miles, leaving his Ford pick-up at home. And the next Christmas he gave me my all-time favorite present – a 14-karat gold lapel pin of the Jaguar emblem.

As my interest in fast cars continued I successfully pitched story ideas to my bosses at *The Journal*: a profile of Knoxville car builder Ed Zink centered on competition at Road Atlanta, then accounts of trips to the 12 Hours of Sebring and the Daytona Continental in Florida and the U.S. Grand Prix at Watkins Glen in New York. A couple of friends who were also gear heads, Tom Stokes and Steve Horne, usually joined me. The following are accounts of some of those trips, with accompanying photos.

Sports Car Club of America

Watching an authoritative-looking official take one of the small cards and hand it to the business-suited man beside him, I decided that I needed to know what those cards were about. The exchange – after a smiling hand-shake – was on the top floor of the press tower at Road Atlanta, and the time was late November 1970.

The relatively new facility was hosting its first Sports Car Club of America's annual championship spectacle, 16 separate races contested over a weekend. The American Road Race of Champions is the national pinnacle of amateur racing, featuring everything from Volkswagen-powered, hand-built open-wheeled single-seaters to souped up sedans to screaming racing vehicles with legendary livery such as Shelby, McLaren and Lola.

My two companions and I were there because I had parlayed my position at *The Journal* into press credentials for the three of us. My badge allowed me just about anywhere. But my friends' access was more limited – I was the only one of us allowed into the press tower's top floor. I was the night news editor and rock 'n' roll critic of *The Journal*, Horne was the night police reporter, and Stokes was a college friend who sometimes read the newspaper. I had managed to get Horne and Stokes credentials as photographers.

So as soon as I had the opportunity – when I was sure no one

With Steve Horne, at Road Atlanta, photo by Tom Stokes

would notice – I checked out the cards. They were invitations to the Datsun Awards Banquet scheduled that night in a fancy hotel near downtown Atlanta. I picked up three and quickly exited the tower. Back on the ground, I handed my companions their invitations.

The three of us had already familiarized ourselves with the paddock and pits area, crossed the bridge to the infield, and made our way to the hill overlooking Turn 5. And I had interviewed our legitimate reason for attending the event. Ed Zink was the most successful builder of Formula Vee racers and the majority of the entrants in that class were his products.

And now we had a good reason to drive into Atlanta when the day's racing was finished. Atlanta, we reasoned, would offer motels where we could find a cheap room.

But the banquet came first, so we made our way to the fancy hotel. After deciding that our clothing was not suitable for such an event, we changed into more presentable shirts and attempted to knock the red-clay dust from our jeans. Horne, who had brought an extra pair of pants, insisted that Stokes and I stand guard while he changed in the dark parking lot.

Inside, we followed the signboards and discovered there were two tables where we could present our invitations. Horne and I went to the first and Stokes the second, our choices later proving significant.

We were in, and we soon discovered that Datsun was sparing no expense – open bars offered bottomless alcohol and waiters and waitresses circulated with hors d'oeuvres featuring shrimp and other fancies. Drinks and dinner, compliments of Datsun.

As we circulated, marveling at our good fortune, we showed our sophistication by switching from beer to cocktails for a round or two. But I had to wince as my companions, alcohol ramping up their confidence, made outrageous claims about Ferraris and Benzes. I reminded them that none of us owned a car that would get us the 200 miles from Knoxville to the track, that we were only there because Dad had loaned me his 1965 Ford station wagon.

Then we noticed that the room was being magically expanded – a wall began to roll open and we discovered that we were going to be seated for dinner, that the appetizers we had been wolfing down were, in fact, only appetizers. We found a table and were seated with a quartet of mechanics – fortunately for us, their knowledge of life's finer offerings was as limited as ours. They, too, brought beers from the bar to accompany their steaks.

We tried to keep up with the technical talk until one of the mechanics included Stokes in the conversation by asking what kind of camera he used. His answer was something along the lines of "depends on the situation." I tried to change the subject with a remark about the juiciness of my steak. Finally, Horne waded in with a comment about Zink's success with the Volkswagen-powered entries and the conversation veered back to their side of the table.

Sobered somewhat by the intake of food, we were relatively alert when the Datsun master of ceremonies took his position at the on-stage microphone to thank us for welcoming Datsun to the U.S. market, for recognizing that their cars were competitive.

And, he added, Datsun wanted to recognize several members of the racing press. "When I call your name, please stand," he said. There was the long-time racing writer for *The New York Times*, someone from *Sports Illustrated*, familiar names from the automative publications – and Tom Stokes from *The Knoxville Journal*.

Stokes stood up and graciously acknowledged the applause with a wave as Horne and I looked on in disbelief. After he sat down and accepted grinning nods from our table companions, Horne and I wanted to know how he managed to get recognition, especially since we actually worked at *The Journal* and he was only with us because we had invited him along.

"When I gave the girl at the table my invitation," he explained, "she wrote down my name and my newspaper."

As the to-do broke up and we headed back to our car to find cheap accommodation, Horne and I came up with a get-even plan. We would rent a room for two – and Stokes would sleep on the floor.

12 Hours of Sebring 1971

The glass of champagne wasn't something I had planned, or even cared much about. But I was standing beside Dick Smothers – half of the Brothers comedy team – and I was not supposed to be there, having crashed the VIPs-only scene. And that made me the envy of my traveling companions, therefore drawing a chuckle at the memory a half century later. The place was Sebring, Florida, and the year was 1971.

While my knack for gaining entrance to places where I am not welcome is handy in the news business, I had actually been swept along to the champagne by circumstances.

I had cadged press credentials for the 12 Hours of Sebring inviting Horne and Stokes along. The three of us had set up our base around my decidedly un-sporty vehicle, a 1962 Chrysler New Yorker equipped with push-button automatic transmission. Its faded look was augmented by a coating of bug carcasses accumulated during our drive from Knoxville, a look that stood out from the other infield vehicles. Its surroundings included fancy campers and cars that looked like they could either compete on the track or were part of race-team support. There was no chance of the Chrysler being confused with the vehicles sporting Ferrari, Porsche and Alfa-Romeo livery.

At race's end, with no idea where Stokes and Horne were, I was mingling with participants and crews behind the pits when I noticed the well-lit VIP tent and the crowd jockeying to get inside. Admittance required the correct credentials – a pair of uniformed Florida Highway Patrolmen stood at the entrance to make sure of

A pair of Porsche 917s exiting the pits at Sebring

legitimacy. Of course I tried to get in, flashing my credentials, but was quickly turned down by the no-nonsense troopers.

Off-track entertainment at Watkins Glen

A couple of bystanders witnessed my attempt and asked what was going on. I told them the constabulary's rules. They scoffed as they were joined by other friends. It seemed they were the Jim Baker racing team, a group from Atlanta with a disdain for the sophisticated European entrants – they raced Corvettes. "I don't think a couple of Florida troopers can stop us," one of them said.

A decision was quickly made and I was invited to join the bull-rush of the troopers. And within a couple of minutes I was drinking champagne with Dick Smothers in the company of such competitors as Derek Bell, Vic Elford, and Mario Andretti. Stokes and Horne? I learned later that they were already asleep.

Other racing trips included covering the Daytona Continental, returns to Sebring and Road Atlanta for a Can-Am competition and a long haul to Watkins Glen, New York for the 1972 U.S. Grand Prix. The Can-Am race featured top drivers and teams – and I was able to elbow my way into the presence of Stirling Moss, who drove the pace car. Watkins Glen is memorable because Stokes and I were foiled as we tried to sleep while patrolling state troopers on horseback kept rousting drunken revelers nearby.

Louisville and the Indianapolis 500

My next memorable encounters in the auto-racing world happened when I was living in Louisville, only 100 miles south of Indianapolis and its famous Brickyard. That meant a couple of trips north – the first time paying attention to the race, the second time careening through the infield crowd with a friend. I had taken a job at *The Louisville Times* after copy-editing stints at *The Miami Herald* and *The Charlotte Observer* and soon was Number 2 in the Times' feature department. I discovered that one of my *Times* cohorts was a motor-head, too. Greg Johnson was the editor of the *Times* Saturday magazine, *Scene*. He was a Hoosier native and had been a frequent visitor to the Indianapolis track.

His personal vehicles during the years I was working with him ranged from Japanese motorcycles to big-block Detroit products to tricked-out German-engineered marvels to a tiny Italian sportscar. But I only rode with him once, in an IROC Camaro – his demonstration of the car's attributes, though skillful, convinced me to decline any subsequent offers of rides around the block.

After my second sortie to the Indy 500, one of the paper's photographers tipped me to the relative sanity of qualifying weekend, and I made pre-Memorial Day visits in subsequent years. Because of my media connections, and because of the gearhead interest of Johnson, I could always come up with an excuse to head to Indianapolis when there was track action.

Then, in the spring of 1980, Johnson heard that an outfit called Malibu Grand Prix was going to open a facility near Louisville. For a couple of dollars per lap, Malibu furnished the track, the cars, and even the helmets. The Malibu vehicles were single-seat open-wheeled cars each outfitted with a 28-horsepower Wankel rotary engine. They were capable of more than 65 miles per hour – a speed that the tight twists of the track did not allow. The lack of a straightaway limited top speeds to 35 or 40 mph.

Naturally, I volunteered for a story. We came up with an experienced amateur driver named Wilson Welch to provide a serious appraisal, and Johnson indulged the delusional approach that I borrowed from James Thurber.

I opened with a quote from Stirling Moss, Formula 1 legend, and one of the great drivers of the sport. Auto racing, Moss had told an interviewer, is "like making love."

My account follows:

First, I forgot my racing jacket, the nylon job with the racing patches – Jaguar on the breast and Daytona Continental 1971 on the left shoulder. Then I was told that I wouldn't need my Nomax flame-resistant underwear. And, since there were no exotic-looking women crowded around the pit area – or even non-exotic-looking women – my allusion to Moss was obviously wishful thinking. How was I going to play big-time Grand Prix driver without my trappings, without an audience? And what about my practiced French accent, mon cherie?

The car sure looked authentic – open-wheeled, rear-engined, big racing slicks wrapped around mean-looking alloy wheels, positively sexy in its gleaming French-racing-blue paint, set off by a few manufacturers' decals.

There was nothing wrong with the track – it had all kinds of turns and twists and hairbrush curves and apexes and lateral drifts and four-wheel slides. It had the thrilling smell of burning fuel, the roar of car engines. And the timing tower, inscrutable and all-knowing. The final word.

And my competition was there. Wilson Welch was a veteran of solos and gymkhanas and the Malibu facility in Columbus, Ohio. And he had remembered to wear his racing jacket. When I arrived, he was already hunched down in his car, helmet in place, seat belt snug.

There were last-minute instructions from the Malibu employees, something about "staying on the course." By the time I was strapped in, Welch was already out, halfway around the track.

I eased up to the light. Red, then the arrow flashed, then yellow, then green. The blue Virage lurched across the starting line, clipped the first corner, clipped the second corner. This, I guessed, is what they called the ragged edge.

Finally, I got the beast under control and threw it into the next turn. And the next. Belatedly, I realized that this beast goes where it is pointed.

That sure made it easier. I screamed around the course, nearly flying off the track and onto my apex only once. Finally I goosed it through the finish line and looked at the timing clock: 78:48. Welch, on his second lap, came through right behind: 59:37. At least he hadn't lapped me.

I looked around to see if anyone had noticed my efforts. Maybe Walter Mitty's cousin was present. But the only witnesses were two sniggering Malibu employees, and they quickly looked away when I glared at them.

Well, by Stirling, I could do better. My next lap was 68.32. Welch's was 58:12. But I had lost time by waving at one of the mechanics when I mistook him for Moss.

My times improved — 66:14, 64:02, 60:00.

Did I smell something burning? Maybe that was my problem – engine trouble. I pitted. The mechanic suggested the smell was from my sweat. "You're working too hard, throwing the car around the curves," he said. "Smoothly, you want to drive smoothly."

I thought I was.

I looked for Welch – he was off the track, his wheels spinning in the grass. At least I hadn't spun out.

I asked about the best time during the night before, when the track opened for a radio-station promotion. Slightly more than 54 seconds, the mechanic said, with a knowing chuckle. But that crowd was made up of rock 'n' roll crazies, I pointed out.

Welch got back on the track, waving as he sped past. I quickly followed, trying to catch him. My times got better, down to 59.88. But Welch turned a 57.33. And that was it. After my sub-minute lap, my times got worse.

But I vowed to practice, to visit the track often. Maybe Welch could give me pointers. Or at least introduce me to a couple of girls …

24 Heures du Mans 1979

Early in 1979, Tom Stokes and I decided we should check into attending the 24-hour race at LeMans, France. I knew that the *Louisville Times Scene* editor Greg Johnson would be an easy sale and an official *Courier-Journal & Times* letterhead request signed by Johnson was soon in the mail, listing me as the reporter, Stokes as the photographer.

The letter of acceptance was soon in hand, with vague instructions on picking up the credentials – in French, of course. We decided that we could figure out the details on the trans-Atlantic flight.

We planned the trip around a two-week vacation, with time in Paris and Boulogne. I wrote my story longhand on the flight back to the U.S. and Johnson published it in *Scene*. This much-improved version is helped by several decades of hindsight, accented with a dose of "I can't believe we managed this…" The photos on the starting grid were taken by Stokes, the others by me.

Paul Newman in the morning rain, early Sunday

On a rainy night in the summer of 1979, I was awakened from a sound sleep by loud laughter followed by a quieter "shhhh". The language was French, the voices female. Quietly turning my head, I could see the lower legs and feet of three women, a trio who did not know they were being observed by two males who had been asleep under the truck where they now stood.

The place was Le Mans, France, and the time was about 4 a.m., approximately 14 hours into the 24 Heures du Mans, one of the world's premier auto-racing events. Though the rain had been steady for several hours, the race continued, the roar of the cars as they thundered past only a couple hundred yards from us delivering aural proof. My friend Tom Stokes and I had found the truck when we were searching for a comfortable and dry place to catch some sleep. It was large and high enough off the ground for our needs.

Our media passes gave us access to the high-security paddock area where trucks and trailers secured and sheltered supplies for the racing teams. The females, we surmised, were somehow associated with one of the teams, which would explain their presence. And, we quickly realized, they were inebriated – and looking for an out-of-the-way place to relieve themselves.

We remained quiet until the girls had departed. Stokes went back to sleep, but I crawled out and found my way to one of the public-access food-and-drink tents in the infield just beyond the pit road. I was hoping it was not too early to find another made-on-the-spot quiche like I had enjoyed earlier. In the tent, a few staffers played host to a handful of guests, only two of whom were awake. Three or four others, heads down on their arms, had succumbed to the late hour.

One still clutched his half-empty beer mug though he was obviously asleep. And another had simply sprawled on top of a table and passed out.

Two waiters were treating themselves with a bottle of cheap champagne. One of the pair had given into his condition, but the other still attempted the elegance of his station – his burgundy jacket buttoned, his black bow tie still tight though his white shirt was spotted with wine stains.

When he saw me, wet and bedraggled, he woke a nearby waitress. She took the interruption of her nap in good humor, managing a smile when she served my coffee, and apologizing when she said it was too early for the quiche. She offered a croissant instead. "Frais du boulangerie," I was assured. The coffee provided much-needed caffeine and the warmth of the croissant did, indeed, affirm its freshness.

But for many of the racing teams, the situation was not champagne and smiles as the day slowly dawned. By 7:30 a.m. only 28 of the original 55 entries were still running.

Stokes and I were veteran automobile-race fans – I had cadged media credentials for the 12 Hours of Sebring, the Daytona Continental, the U.S. Grand Prix, the Indianapolis 500 and several events at Road Atlanta. Equipped with one of my cameras, Stokes would pretend that he knew how to use it.

My present job at *The Louisville Times* meant that I could often parlay my racing interest into assignments for Greg Johnson, a Times editor whose love for speed on wheels was such that I was wary of riding with him. Johnson had quickly assured me that if I could get to Le Mans, he would publish my story, especially since the '79 race would feature an added attraction in the actor Paul Newman, who at age 54 was still a formidable racing competitor. He and his teammates were driving a Porsche 935 Turbo. With 20 on the starting grid, the 935 was the era's make and model of choice.

After the start of the race – before the rains came – Stokes and I had wandered around, getting a feel for the scene. The route includes several miles of public road (closed during the race, of course) and the infield encompasses several acres of farmland. The circuit is more than 11 miles long, which means the infield is vast, large enough to hold thousands of camping fans, huge tents for food and drink, an automotive museum, and booths and more elaborate set-ups where automobiles and their ancillary products were on display.

In some areas of the infield, off-limits to fans, French country life went on as usual. A few hundred feet inside the Tetre Rouge, the turn that leads into the Mulsanne Straight, a farmer was busy working his fields seemingly unaware of the cars hurtling down the straight at more than 220 miles per hour.

As the rain had begun and the sky darkened, fans grabbed whatever shelter was available. Dim, sodden lumps were visible under trees and bushes or huddled beneath concessionaires' overhangs. Some usurped space in closed-for-the-night display booths. The pedestrian tunnel under the track had filled quickly. The fans who were prescient – or just lucky – had escaped to rented rooms in town. The seats they had abandoned that were in the covered grandstands were soon filled by fans able to sneak in as the ticket-takers sought shelter themselves.

The privileged, those connected with racing teams and the sponsors, fared better. The paddock area was filled with camping trailers and trucks. There, by-invitation-only clubs hosted parties that went on through most of the night. The three sets of female legs had probably wandered away from one of those gatherings.

After Stokes had joined me in the tent, when the sun began to peek out of a clearing sky, we made our way through the pedestrian tunnel into the now-quiet carnival area, finding seats in the grandstand that provided an excellent vantage point for photos with the pits in the background on the other side of the track. But as the seat holders returned to the stands, fortified with coffee and their expensive tickets, we had to give up our seats.

Paul Newman and Dick Barbour with the Hawaiian Tropic girls

Minutes earlier, I tried to talk the Hawaiian Tropic girls in to posing for me

As the carnival area slowly re-opened, we noticed the kinds of attractions not seen at U.S. fairs in several years: sword-swallowers, Rita the fat lady, freak shows featuring exhibits such as two-headed dogs, opportunities to win a prize by besting a strongman. And, appropriate for Le Mans, daredevils who seemingly defy gravity racing around the sides of a cylindrical track.

We made our way back through the pedestrian tunnel and claimed seats in a media-only area above the pits, a prime position for the 2 p.m. checkered flag. Not surprisingly, the winners drove a 935 Turbo, but they were not veterans of the circuit. American brothers Don and Bill Whittington and their co-driver, German Klaus Ludwig, claimed the prize. The Whittingtons had begun their serious racing efforts only

18 months earlier. Newman and his veteran partners, Dick Barbour and Rolf Stommelman, finished second.

As the bottles of champagne flowed along pit row, as fans tried to get a clear view of Paul Newman, Stokes and I, wet and worn out, made our way to the station for the train trip back to Paris, soon to be lulled to sleep by the rail-clacking rhythm.

Wandering Again, 2010

On the way to classes in Cyprus, via Florida (without Mickey Mouse) and a cruise ship full of vacationing Brits, including stops in Bermuda, Portugal and Belgium. Special appearances by motorcyclists in the Peloponnese, goatherders in Larnaca, and camel jockeys in Cairo.

In 2010, I agreed to accompany eight University of Tennessee students on a study-abroad program in Cyprus. Faculty member Bob Legg and I would spend four weeks teaching two classes – I would oversee the students as they created travel blogs and Legg would lead them in making a documentary film.

Our students – juniors and seniors, seven female, one male – would represent several disciplines: journalism, communication studies, political science, business.

I don't like to fly, so I decided to turn the trip into an adventure. Eventually, I settled on boarding a cruise ship in Miami for a two-week sail to Harwich, England with stops in Bermuda, Lisbon and Bruges.

From England I would travel to Paris via the Chunnel train, then more rail journeys, Paris to Milan to Bari for an overnight ferry to Patras, Greece. After spending time in the Peloponnese before several days in Athens, I would then fly to Larnica, Cyprus, where I would meet the rest of the group when they arrived.

We would be domiciled in Nicosia, the capital of the Republic of Cyprus, the Greek-speaking southern side of the island, still divided after a conflict with Turkey that began in the early 1960s. There is a demilitarized zone between the two sides that is administered by the United Nations.

The students would meet for classes on some days; other days would be built around field trips for stories that would be part of both the blogs and the film.

I would be on the island for five weeks, and out of the U.S. for 11 weeks.

I would set out from Miami on a cruise ship. I worked at *The Miami Herald* in 1973 and '74, so I use my experience then as the set-up for my return to the city in 2010. Except for the newsroom picture, the accompanying photos were taken by me.

Miami 1973

When I went to work at *The Miami Herald* in the early1970s, the newspaper was my introduction to big-time journalism, Miami my first foray into big-city life. *The Herald* then was fat with pages and news and ambition. Besides several metro-Miami editions, there were a half-dozen aimed at different sections of the state, plus two for Latin America that were flown each night to Rio de Janeiro, Buenos Aires, Caracas.

New York City journalism had recently experienced a major upheaval with several of the dailies closing, sending dozens of staffers heading south for jobs in Florida. Many landed at *The Herald*, adding to what was already a diverse group of wily veterans, including a refugee or two from pre-Castro Havana.

There was Gene Miller, two-time winner of the Pulitzer Prize for investigative work. When he was present, his loud and dogged phone interviews dominated the newsroom.

At the other end of the spectrum was Edna Buchanan, her demure appearance belying her skill with grisly stories from the police beat; and Jay Maeder, whose laconic demeanor masked a rapier wit that eventually found fruition in a column.

Jim Dance, a talented and eccentric editorial writer, introduced himself a few days after I started work. He was a fellow native of southern Appalachia, from Middlesboro, Kentucky. His brother had been mayor of Knoxville.

Then there was Ben Hunt, a Brit who had been declared *persona non grata* in Ian Smith's Rhodesia for refusing to vote, a requirement for all white residents. He had worked for papers in London, Johannesburg, and Toronto.

It was an interesting mix, making for an interesting publication.

At that time, South Beach wasn't exactly seedy, but it was years removed from today's glitz. The atmosphere was traditional beach-boardwalk. A Coney Island habitué would have felt at home – and many of them had fled Brooklyn for Florida's warmer climes.

The south end of the beach gave way to a greyhound-racing track. Many of its patrons were regulars at a bar/restaurant a half block away. The Turf was dark and smoky, an escape from the sun, sand and surf just across Collins Avenue. It was close enough to *The Herald* via MacArthur Causeway that it became one of our regular dinner-break spots. Our usual waitress was a Brooklyn escapee with an accent that was thicker than the burgers.

Another favorite, within walking distance of *The Herald* on Biscayne Boulevard, was the Lobo Lounge, a place that could have been a mainstay of many Brooklyn neighborhoods.

But most often after work we headed a few miles up Biscayne Boulevard to the North Dade Athletic Club, where the only athletic equipment was a pool table and a Pong machine. The hours were the main attraction – as a private club ($2 to join), it stayed open until 3 a.m.

The Herald building was on Biscayne Bay, which meant spectacular views from the east-facing windows. We could watch the seaplanes of Chalk Airlines as they landed on the water. Or the Goodyear blimp, tethered next door to the Chalk facility on Watson Island. In the accompanying photo, I'm the bearded editor in the middle handing copy to the news editor.

A bit farther south from the newspaper building there were usually several cruise ships tied at the Port of Miami pier. I would soon be boarding one of the successors to those ships, but not before checking out the old *Herald* neighborhood. I'm sure my favorite spots have changed, my old haunts have disappeared, the tropical funk replaced by sparkle and glamour. Nevertheless, I am looking forward to seeing Miami again.

*The Herald newsroom;
I'm the bearded guy in the middle distance*

Miami, again

In South Georgia, Interstate 75 billboards dominate the terrain, touting pecans, peaches, peanuts. Closer to Tifton, just beyond the sign boosting the "historic" downtown, spa advertisements take over – there is Lucky Spa, No. 1 Spa, Tokyo Spa (Truckers Welcome). South Georgia is, it appears, about more than fruit and nuts.

Across the state line, roadside scenery quickly changes. North Florida apparently has stricter rules when it comes to billboards. They are there, but not in such numbers. Real estate, a classic Florida sell, is touted, at least until horse country starts. Then the interstate cuts through expensive terrain, home to thoroughbred horses and their moneyed owners. Billboards, apparently, aren't as welcome.

Ocala comes and goes as a fierce thunderstorm hits, then I take the tollway heading east, horse culture giving way to Mouse culture as Orlando looms. I skirt Disney country to the south, leaving its tourist attractions to those more enamored of rodents and their fascist creators than I am. Back into desolate agriculture country, finally leaving the turnpike for a room in Okeechobee.

The next morning, I head east for Interstate 95, making contact in Palm Beach County at rush hour. Just before 8 a.m. two guys in a convertible speed around me, top down, golf clubs filling up the back seat. This is the Florida I remember.

On the outskirts of Miami, I get off I-95 in favor of Biscayne Boulevard. Little River, where I briefly lived before leaving Miami, is now a Caribbean enclave, a Little Haiti with its bright colors, street-front food vendors and storefronts blaring reggae – or on one occasion, Aretha Franklin. But the seeming prosperity is only evident for a couple of blocks; empty buildings and caved-in roofs speak to a desperate poverty only a few steps off the main drag.

Right onto 36th to see what remains of the North Dade Athletic Club. There's the building, sadly boarded up and graffiti-splattered. Not surprising, as the joint's heyday was 35 years ago.

On to downtown, where new high rises crowd Biscayne Bay. *The Herald* is still where it was when I worked there – but part of the building is rented to a school. Across the MacArthur Causeway to South Beach. No dogtrack, no Turf Bar, just sleek, airy hipster hangouts instead. But the pedestrian traffic seems to be the same mix, enough recent retirees to offset the weathered beach habituees who have called it home for decades.

And just south of the causeway, tied up at the Port of Miami, is my ship, the Jewel of the Seas. Time to ditch the car and board the boat.

As the ship slips through Governor's Cut, South Beach to the left, Miami is spectacular in the rear-view mirror, like most cities beautiful from a distance, not so much from street level. After all, Miami is a tropical metropolis, sunny funkiness edging toward heat-induced rot.

At Sea

The last time I was on board a boat out of Miami, it was a 12-foot Sunfish, property of a fellow *Herald* employee named Dave Finley. It was my first adventure on a sailboat, and it ended with the Sunfish on its side in the Atlantic off Key Biscayne, Finley and I thrashing around trying to right it as a Coast Guard Albatross circled overhead. We finally got it upright, clambered aboard, and returned to the safety of Biscayne Bay.

The Jewel of the Seas is a bit more of a boat – a cruise ship of the Royal Caribbean line, a gleaming, massive party vessel with a full casino, a theater, several restaurants and bars, two swimming pools, a library, resident acts ranging from magic to musical, and, not to be discounted, two ping-pong tables.

The passengers, headed for Harwich, England, with stops in Bermuda, Lisbon, and Bruges, number about 3,000. Judging from their destination-tagged T-shirts and tote bags, they are a well-traveled bunch: All the expected Caribbean locations, plus the Falklands, Cape Horn, K2 Pakistan, the Black Sea. When a destination is featured on a T-shirt, it's no longer remote no matter how far away it may seem.

The British seem to be in the majority, many headed home after South Florida vacations. Out of Miami, weather hot and humid, the outdoor pool is popular, tanners catching the rays. The female regulars at the poolside tableau could have starred in an R. Crumb fantasy, at least in their younger day. The first few days, before we head north into cooler weather, the pool is the center of activity, with line-dance lessons, bean-bag toss, a putting contest, and the World Male Belly-Flop Championship. The last garners everyone's attention when a female, helped by libations from the Pool Bar, insists on entering fully clothed. She competes, but loses out to a big-bellied Scotsman.

Shameless Brits at poolside on the Jewel of the Seas

My dining tablemates – Peggy, Sandy, and Rosa – are all cruise veterans and, natives of the New Orleans area, not easily fooled when it comes to eats. Even as we critique what Royal Caribbean is serving up, we are talking about the best of the Crescent City. I learn to always insist on unwashed oysters (saltier and tastier); that in real Italian households, tomato sauce is called "red gravy;" and that the best bread pudding is found at the Red Maple in Gretna.

On Mother's Day, we hit Bermuda, though many are disappointed because downtown Hamilton and its shopping is closed, it being Sunday.

After eight hours ashore, it is back at sea – five days until Lisbon. As we are farther north, it is generally too chilly for much poolside activity, though the solarium pool is still available for the serious water sportsmen. So the two ping-pong tables, wind-protected in the verandah, start drawing crowds.

When I take my tea, I can watch ping-pong. There are even formal-wear games. (Several evenings are designated for formal wear – I do not participate but am startled one night by a huge Scotsman in tux and kilt, a sight not soon forgotten.)

One of the appeals of a cruise is that it can be an escape. You are among folks that you never have to see again; you can participate in belly-flop competitions in anonymity; you can spend hours in the casino without anyone (except your banker) knowing about it; you can take the stage on amateur night and pretend you're on "American Idol."

And, like the man in the kilt, dress however you want.

One Brit, bald and in his 50s, favors an all-red outfit. His sleeveless shirt, mid-calf pants (they used to be called pedal-pushers), and matching Keds wouldn't be acceptable in any London office, even on casual Friday.

Finally, Lisbon looms. I sign up for a shore excursion to a national park and fishing village south of the city. There is a stop at the Fonseca winery, where I discover that one of their products is an old favorite from my undergraduate days, Lancers wine. On the tour, Most-Obnoxious title goes to a couple who insist on loudly arguing with each other in the middle of our guide's commentary.

The coastal scenery is spectacular, wildflowers in bloom, blue sea below. The tortuous cliffside roads remind me of those short States-side news stories: 56 die when bus plunges down Portuguese mountainside. Fortunately, our driver is experienced, his bus in top shape.

Back on board, next stop Bruges. I haven't been there, but I have spent a lot of time in Brussels and am way too familiar with Belgian chocolate, so I am looking forward to grabbing a supply to get me across Europe.

And I want to see the Michelangelo sculpture housed in the Church of Our Lady. The sculpture, Madonna at Bruges, is reason enough to visit Belgium. Because it's in a church and not a museum, there is no crowd when I visit; I can spend as much time as I want admiring the work of a master.

There is also success on the chocolate front – I pick up a kilo and head back to the ship. The next stop is the port of Harwich, then a short train ride to London followed by a taxi trip across the city to St. Pancras Station for the EuroStar, the luxurious Chunnel train that connects London and Paris in less than two hours.

Another taxi-ride, this time across Paris, Gare de Nord to Gare de Bercy, and an overnight train to Milano. As I've done in the past, I wake in the middle of the night and peer out the window at the quiet Simplon Pass train station of Brig before continuing into Italy. A few hours later, I am awakened by the conductor announcing Milano.

Italy & the Adriatic

The Milano train station at 6 a.m. is quiet, and my train for Bari, a primary port on the Adriatic Sea, doesn't leave until 7:35. So I find a spot to sit. Unfortunately, the only place I can find is Smokers' Corner, so I periodically put up with tobacco, the Indians' Revenge.

As rush hour approaches, the station starts to get busy and I move to where I can see the schedule to find out the platform where I'll board. I notice a black man, carrying a large bag, as he keeps traipsing around a circle of his own making. Then he puts down his bag next to a light pole, and goes back to his circling. By now there are a lot of commuters coming and going.

Suddenly the black man starts hollering as he walks, his comments in a dialect that only he understands. The other schedule watchers start watching him as well. A passing policeman, typical of Italian officialdom, studiously ignores him.

Finally, my train shows up on the schedule list and I make my way to Platform 12. I'm in seat 54, car 2. I find car 2, but its seat numbers stop at 32. So I plop down in the nearest empty seat and stow my bags overhead.

As we pull out, four train officials claim the spots across the aisle and another passenger, also unable to find his reserved seat, questions them. They wave him off. So I stay put since the car is not crowded and plenty of seats are available.

But as we get closer to Bologna, the train gains more commuters at each stop. I have to move twice as passengers claim my seat. At least I'm able to stay in the vicinity of my bags so I don't have to pull them down for relocation.

East of Bologna the crowd thins as we speed through vineyards toward the Adriatic. At Ancona, we swing south and head down the coast.

Train-station splendor in Milan

The towns are beach escapes, some with sleek new resort hotels, others with older, funkier facilities. Blue sky, blue sea, palms swaying in the breeze – interesting ride, until all the towns start to blur together.

I am scheduled to catch a 10 p.m. ferry at Bari, an over-nighter for Patras, Greece with stops in Corfu and Igoumenitsa. The train is scheduled to arrive at Bari at 3:35 p.m. We make it at about 6, during a downpour. I'm beginning to understand the contention that Mussolini was popular in Italy solely because he made the trains run on time. And I'm glad I've got until 10 p.m.

At the port, I don't have to worry with Italian officialdom – there isn't any. Nor signs. But there are a large number of wet motorcyclists, apparently together and heading for Patras, too. With the help of the ferry folks, I find my way to customs and the ship. Pulling my bag, dodging puddles and tractor-trailer trucks pulling up into the boat, I make it aboard and am shown my room.

The facilities are nice, much better than I expected for a ferry. But I soon discover that the smokers have the run of the ship, and most of the bikers are smokers. The bikers, male and female, are Harley-Davidson riders, sporting gear with home-club information on the back. They are from Poland, Sweden, Slovakia, Germany, Denmark.

In the dining room cafeteria line, I opt for pastitsia, the Greek pasta casserole, and a salad. The servings are huge. Not paying attention to signage, I sit down in a section marked "Welcome Truckers" and soon find myself in conversation with a German driver from Hanover on his way to Kalamata, Greece, with a load of furniture. Our neighbors are two Dutch drivers and five guys from Romania. All have massive plates of fries that they cover with massive amounts of mayonnaise. The bikers display similar culinary tastes.

The German speaks fair English, and translates for the other guys, all of whom speak some German. I ask why they drive through Italy and take the ferry across instead of traveling through the Balkans. The answer is quick – it's less expensive because they don't have to stop every 100 kilometers and pay a bribe, which they tell me is the norm through the Balkans.

When the others return to their fries and mayo, the German explains that many of the southern Europeans who immigrated north for employment after World War II want to return to their birthplace when they retire: "They want to take their possessions with them." So he makes furniture runs.

Then he confides that he only does this about once a month, that he's old enough to retire. With a wink, he adds, "I have reasons not to stay at home."

After the German takes his bottle of wine and retires, and the bikers get heavily into their cigarettes and Carlsbergs, I return to my stateroom and hit the sack, sleeping through Corfu and Igoumenitsa. I wake as we maneuver into port at Patras – three days and three countries, by train and by boat.

Run to Olympia

I don't plan to spend much time in Patras – basically I want to get to the station and catch the train for Olympia, about 100 miles south. Olympia was the site of the ancient Olympics, described in the travel literature as an "idyllic glade" surrounding the ruins of the games' facilities.

It's also well off the beaten track. From Patras, the rail route is to Pyrgos, a center of the farming community that comprises this part of the Peloponnese. There's a train change at Pyrgos for the short trip inland to the site where Olympic athletes competed every four years for more than 1,100 years.

As I make my way to the Patras station, a few hundred yards from the ferry dock, I notice that my Harley friends have been joined by scores of their buddies. There are motorcycles everywhere. Then I find that the last train to Olympia – there are three daily – departed at about 11:30 a.m. It's now about 3 p.m. Next train is tomorrow at 6 a.m., with the second at 9.

I walk out of the station, pulling and carrying my luggage as I dodge Harleys to cross the street. Luckily, there is a vacancy at the first hotel I walk into, the Astir, a large, well-kept edifice that looks to have been built in the 1920s.

Tomorrow, Saturday, will be the day for my Olympic run. Later, exploring, I discover that Patras is hosting a Europe-wide Harley-Davidson rally. The riders number in the thousands and they dominate the city. Greek kids are mesmerized by the big bikes, some of the more adventuresome clambering aboard for photos. I don't see any get caught by bike owners, most of whom I'm sure would not be amused.

The next day, I make the 9 a.m. train for Olympia. There are three cars. We ramble out of Patras, through a trackside slum that seems to be occupied mostly by black Africans. Next is an intensely cultivated agriculture area. There are expanses of olive trees, with citrus interspersed, fields of tomatoes and melons and cucumbers, and, of course, vineyards. The towns are small and clustered around tiny train stations. The only roads are dirt.

Finally, we reach Pyrgos and I get off for the short hop to Olympia. This time, there are only two cars. Besides a couple of Greeks who apparently have gone into Pyrgos for supplies, the only other passengers are a Dutch tourist couple.

The train stops wherever the Peloponnese want to get on or off, whether there is a station or not. The driver seems to know his passengers and where they want to disembark. He stops at one dirt road to pick up a woman and her child, then lets them off at the next dirt road, maybe a quarter mile away. No one ever asks her for a ticket.

At another crossing, he stops to trade jokes with two acquaintances, and then continues. This train is truly a local.

Finally, Olympia. By this point the Dutch couple are my only fellow passengers. The town is tourist-oriented, but still quiet and quaint, only four or five blocks long, with residences arrayed around a hill overlooking it.

The ruins and accompanying museum are a short walk away, occupying space between two streams. The museum contains several true masterpieces, in a country where such relics are commonly unearthed. And yet it is uncrowded, though several busloads of tourists are present. I will appreciate my time here later when I've been hurried and harried through Athens museums.

Outside are the remains of the gymnasium, the stadium, the baths, and the temple of Zeus (original home of one of the 7 Wonders of the Ancient World, the sculptor Phidias' statue of the god), as well as a dozen or so other buildings. One was Phidias's workshop. There, archeologists unearthed a cup that is inscribed, "I belong to Phidias."

An Olympian thunderstorm cuts short my visit and I return to the museum, taking shelter in its garden.

A modern storm rolls in on ancient ruins at Olympia

Time is short, and I return to the train station, where I'm soon joined by my Dutch friends. The two-car train returns to Pyrgos in the post-storm sunshine and I'm faced with two hours before the train back to Patras. During the wait, I realize that no matter how exotic the locale might seem, Saturday afternoon in small towns is the same everywhere. The quiet is broken only by songbirds and church bells as everyone rests up for Saturday night.

On the trip to Patras, we pass groups of families and neighbors gathered in back yards alongside the dirt roads and the train tracks, tables and chairs pulled out in yards, games of backgammon and cards contested by adults, soccer balls being kicked by children.

Chromed excess dominates in Patras

Later, back in the middle of the bikers at Patras, I enjoy dinner at a taverna on the pedestrian walkway that dominates the downtown area, watching the motorcyclists as they posture and puff on cigars. A Harley club from Athens has taken over a nearby group of tables. It is dominated by two older men with much-younger female companions, females who have the appearance of being expensive to maintain, much like their chrome chargers.

The next day, as the bikes stream out and as the city cleans up from its busy and noisy weekend, I head to the train station, Athens-bound.

Athens

Our journey for Greece-proper begins by rail, four or five cars headed northeast out of Patras toward Corinth. To the right are hillsides covered by vineyards or olive-tree expanses. To the left are steep drops to the Ionian Sea, the occasional sienna-tiled house perched on a cliffside. But the great Grecian transformation for the 2004 Olympic Games is still under way six years after the event, and the tracks end in a jumble of construction material midway to Corinth. We transfer to a bus, with seats that are more comfortable and air conditioning that is more effective.

Soon, the spectacular Rion-Antirion Bridge looms ahead, spanning the Gulf of Corinth to the mountains of Sterea Erada.

Our bus ride ends about an hour later when we are discharged at a new rail station. The train isn't due yet, and the rail personnel disappear into their own quarters, leaving the rest of us to mill around on the platform. Two fellow passengers quickly distinguish themselves.

The first is a middle-aged man who takes exception to something a male teen has said or done and begins yelling at him. There is pushing and shoving. A passenger informs the railroad officials, who come out of their office and watch. But they do nothing. Finally, the man disappears, still yelling.

A few minutes later another teen, at the other end of the platform, becomes belligerent toward the woman with whom he is sharing a bench. He finally stalks off. Later, on the train, he will again create a scene, this time with his girlfriend. He is a brawl looking for a place to happen, and everyone tries to ignore him.

On the outskirts of Athens, a middle-aged man and a student-aged girl sit down across from me. The man, speaking passable English, proceeds in academic terms to regale the student with his views on mobile-phone use. The Greek woman sitting next to me, who is carrying on a conversation via her mobile phone, has apparently reminded him of a pet communications peeve: He doesn't approve of cell-phone use. The talker can't understand his English and is too engaged in her conversation to pay any attention: Communication about a communication theory in the face of communication reality.

Finally, Athens station, surprisingly small. A short taxi ride and I am at the Cecil Hotel, one of those old European stops with a small entry way almost hidden between street-level shops. The elevator is an ancient cage model, suitable for a role in a 1930s Hitchcock movie.

But the room is clean and comfortable, and the Cecil perfectly located for my purposes, only a couple of blocks from the bustling Monastiraki area and, in the other direction, Omonia Square, the present-day business center. Omonia's ancient equivalent, the Agora, is within walking distance, as are a major flea market, the city's main fresh-food market, and Psiri, site of restaurants, nightclubs, plus, I will find, some of the more unsavory aspects of big-metropolis life.

I discover excellent chocolates at Anassa, where the proprietor asks my help when she finds that I am from the U.S. She wants to know how to pronounce "pecan", an ingredient in one of her favorite offerings.

Then I arrange to join a bus tour that will culminate with the National Archeological Museum and the Acropolis. Neither disappoints.

The entry walkway to the museum features glass flooring revealing the active archeological digs below. Inside, it's masterpiece after masterpiece. But one area stands out because it is empty – the space reserved for the return of the Elgin Marbles from London's British Museum, source of friction between the two countries for decades.

The hill, despite the onslaught of tourists, the babble of guides explaining in a myriad of languages, the restoration work off to one side, dwarfs everything I've seen so far on this trip – even the hundreds of Harley-Davidsons at Patras, its classic lines a simple rebuttal to chromed excess.

The next evening I find a concert at Monastiraki Square, a six-piece brass band, its middle-aged members in black pants and

Music at Monastiraki, lead vocalist the pooch on the right

white shirts, a horn case set out for donations. A crowd gathers, and an unexpected vocalist joins in – a large white dog sings along with the saxophone player. He's a hit.

A Romani woman circulates through the crowd with her hand out, implying that she is collecting for the band members. The tuba player confronts her and a loud argument ensues. The show obviously over, audience members disperse after dropping a few euros into the horn case. And the vocalist wanders over to the edge of the square and stretches out in his usual spot, saving his voice for the next show.

The next day I grab an outdoor table at a taverna on tiny Iroon Square. After perfectly cooked fish with a delicate sauce of sweet peppers and tomatoes, I wander into Psiri, past homeless men sleeping in the entryways of abandoned buildings. Just beyond a small church, I glance down at movement between two parked cars and see a junkie crouched on the curb, shooting up.

Early the next morning I go through Monastiraki, take a quick tour of Hadrian's Library, meet Hadrian's three cats and his tortoise, and climb the hill toward an entrance to the Agora, onetime hangout of Socrates, Aristotle, Demosthenes, Paul and other ancient thinkers.

Along the way, on a quiet side street, is the office of the Melina Mercouri Foundation, the late actor's organization to promote European arts and culture.

The Agora is quiet, a true park of several acres stretching down the northeastern side of the Acropolis and home to another museum of splendid antiquities. Among the ancient Greek ruins is a pacific 11th-century Orthodox church tucked among old trees. But the gem of the park is the Hephaesteion, a temple from 400 BC, and one of the best-preserved edifices in Greece.

Atop a hill, it rises from surrounding greenery, a refuge in the chaotic world that is modern Athens. In fact, only a mile or so away, demonstrations have been taking place against Greece's government and the austerity measures being implemented to help solve the country's economic woes. Perhaps an ancient philosopher or two could help.

The few euros I'm spending aren't going to make much difference, and it's time to head for another country whose roots are in Mycenaean culture, Cyprus.

Cyprus

Mustapha makes his living serving traditional foods of Cyprus – souvlaki, kebab, sheftalia – on Ledra Street, in the Old City of Nikosia, the island's capital. His café is only a few yards from the Green Line, the United Nations demarcation that has divided Cyprus since 1974. His business is on the Turkish side.

Many of Mustapha's customers are tourists who have obtained "visas" from the Turkish Republic of Northern Cyprus to cross from the Republic of Cyprus, the Greek-speaking southern side. The "visas," handed out at a counter just inside northern Cyprus, are recognized only by Turkey. To the rest of the island, and to most of the world, Mustapha's home is characterized as Occupied Cyprus.

On our first full day in Nikosia, we were seated at an outside table at Mustapha's for lunch when I noticed the faded tattoo that adorns Mustapha's right arm – a wolf howling at a crescent moon. When asked, Mustapha explains that the howling wolf is the symbol of the Turkish army, and it adorns his arm because he was part of the force that invaded Cyprus in 1974, over-running and taking control of almost half the island before the U. N. was able to broker a peace. Mustapha moved his family from Turkey and created a life in Nicosia.

These days, he has no problems with visitors from the republic who cross the Green Line. "They are all my friends," he told us.

Our students settled in at Mustapha's café on the occupied side of Cyprus

The invasion, its divisions, and Mustapha's assimilation are only the most recent chapters in centuries of conflicts and occupying armies in Cyprus. The island's strategic location at the eastern end of the Mediterranean has proven irresistible since writers began noticing and taking notes. A diner at Mustapha's only has to glance down the street to see one of the more majestic examples of the island's turbulent past, the Selimiye mosque.

The mosque's twin minarets are visible from most places in the Old City, but from Mustapha's, the viewer can see that they tower above Gothic arches. And that the building next door, now a museum, boasts Gothic gargoyles. The buildings were constructed in the 13th and 14th centuries, when Cyprus was controlled by the Lusignans, Roman Catholics from what is now part of France. The church was consecrated as St. Sophia and was modeled on buildings in papal Europe.

The Ottomans took over in 1570, refurbished the cathedral and turned it into a mosque. But parts of the original building date to even older faiths – three classic columns incorporated for interior support were salvaged from the ruins of Salamis, the island's major eastern port from the 6th century BC until the 8th century AD. During its time, Salamis was ruled by Greeks, Persians, Romans, Ottomans and others, including Venetians, during that city-state's powerful hold on the

The class lined up for a photo at the "birthplace" of Venus

eastern Mediterranean. Nikosia's Venetian Wall still defines the capital's old quarter.

During our four weeks on the island, we will visit ruins from each religion and its cults. And we will discover that Aphrodite, the Greek goddess of love, made the strongest and most lasting impression on the island. In travel brochures touting Cyprus, the "island of Aphrodite" is probably the most popular descriptive phrase. The goddess's "birthplace" on the rocky southwest coast between Limissol and Paphos is a must stop for tourists. That's where the accompanying photo was taken.

Love and religion may have played key roles in the island's ancient history, but for the last couple of centuries military strategy has dominated. From 1878 to 1960, the island was part of the British Empire, providing a staging point for its Mideastern and North African interests. That influence is still paramount, at least on the republic side. The British maintain two vast military bases, English is the island's second language, driving is on the left English-style, and Brits dominate the tourist trade.

But Brits aren't the only Europeans who find Cyprus attractive – thanks to the collapse of the Soviet Union in the late 1980s, you're as likely to hear Russian on the streets as any other language. Dozens of Russian companies are officially incorporated in the republic thanks to friendly regulations. On our 2010 visit we noticed the production facilities of a Russian-language television station and a magazine centered on the "Russian-Cypriot lifestyle." And there are concerns among European Union countries (the republic is a member) that the island's banks have become safe depositories of ill-gotten gains for the crime lords of Russia and the Balkan countries.

During our 2010 visit two episodes reflecting the island's role in the Mideast's constant intrigue and conflict made international news: Limissol was the departure port for a flotilla of ships full of military aid for Gaza that was attacked by Israeli troops, resulting in the deaths of 10 Palestinian activists. And, when several Russians were arrested in the U.S. and accused of spying, the search for their paymaster ended in Cyprus. That person, if he existed, was not apprehended. Speculation in Nicosia was that he had slipped into the occupied side and made his way to Turkey, then across the always-porous Armenian border and on to Moscow, a fitting scenario for an island that has seen such intrigues for centuries.

Sunshine and financial services may be the latest commercial attractions of Cyprus, but the island has provided important products for Europe and the Mideast for centuries. A copper-mining industry based in the central mountain area is still in operation, some of the shafts dating to Roman times.

Much of the copper was transported to the eastern ports of Salamis and Famagusta by camel caravan, and we spent some time in one of its vestiges, a popular tourist destination on the Turkish side of Nicosia. The Buyuk Han is a caravanserai dating to medieval times, its two-story walls providing protection from marauding brigands for the camels, the copper, and the caravans' operators. The han has been restored, its walls again encompassing cafes and shops as they did hundreds of years ago, but the doors are now open, welcoming tourists.

Though there are no camel caravans today, they were still common on the island in the early 1950s when the English writer Lawrence Durrell was a resident. In "Bitter Lemons," his definitive book on the country's inexorable move from British control to independence during that decade, he makes casual mention of passing them when motoring from his home near the northern coast to his government office in Nicosia.

Today, the windswept ruins of the caravans' destination, Salamis, are a tourist destination boasting a Roman amphitheater and baths, along with dozens of statues of Greek and Roman deities, all headless thanks to the Christian zealots who took their turn as occupiers. Both Salamis and Famagusta, the present-day port a few miles south, are on the occupied side.

Not far from Salamis is another example of the Cypriot mash-up, the monastery of St. Barnabas, a Greek Orthodox facility until the invading Turks took it over in 1974. Now it's a museum, with a perfunctory collection of antiquities from Salamis. But the interior sports one of the religious world's most unusual incongruities. Capitals taken from Greek and Roman columns are set in the interior walls, corners

Modern transportation at a 2000-year-old grave

protruding. The result is arresting – Orthodox icons stare at walls studded with triangular reminders of a period when other gods were recognized.

A few yards from the monastery lies the tomb of Saint Barnabas, discovered according to Orthodox tradition in 478 AD by Anthemios, the archbishop of Constantia. The tomb has been a pilgrimage destination ever since. Today's pilgrims arrive by tour bus, take in the quiet flower gardens within the monastery courtyard, and walk down to the tomb. During my 2010 visit, a young European woman in bright-red hotpants lingered on the centuries-old stone steps, providing sore temptation to Barnabas's remains in his final resting place.

After the harbor of Salamis silted up, Famagusta (Ammohostos to the Greeks) became the island's next eastern port. As such, the city became the last refuge of the Crusaders when they were driven from the Holy Land in 1302. Like Nicosia, it, too, boasts a Venetian Wall and mosques that began life as Roman Catholic cathedrals, notably Lala Mustapha Pasa, completed in 1326. It was modeled on the cathedral of Rheims and was consecrated as St. Nicholas.

Famagusta was still in its heyday when the 1974 invasion came, its beaches a popular destination for northern Europeans. The tourist area, Varosia, was primarily owned and operated by Greeks. But in '74, as the Turkish army advanced against token opposition, the Varosians fled their homes and businesses for the south.

After the residents' departure, the Turkish army barricaded Varosia with barbed wire and barrels. By 2010, the neighborhood's once-grand houses were crumbling, home only to rats, cats and snakes. We found the area off-limits to all but the Turkish military, a decaying reminder of Cyprus' modern-day political follies. The most visible remnant in 2010 was a multi-story apartment building, one side sloughing off in collapse.

Varosia's business owners adapted. The once-sleepy fishing village of Agia Napa, 20 miles down the coast – and on the Greek side – has mushroomed into a glitzy parody of a beach resort in only three decades. Dozens of fancy waterfront hotels and attendant bars and restaurants testify to the island's continued appeal as a sunny escape. Many of the spots sport an English-pub atmosphere, and the restaurants feature a world of cuisines. Franchises of U.S.-based restaurants such as TGI Fridays, KFC, and Pizza Hut have gotten into the action, too, joining branches of British betting parlors. All are fed by a 24-hour party mindset.

Many residents still remember the quieter times. One restaurateur, while glad of his tourist business, expressed regret that the Agia Napa of his youth no longer exists. Then, he said, "everyone knew everyone."

And all the dining options aren't ersatz English and American. Vassos, a harborside taverna that has been operating since 1962, serves fresh seafood in an unpretentious, fishing-village atmosphere. The Mediterranean breeze, the cheerful employees, and the delicious food and wine make it easy to ignore the party boats coming and going in the harbor.

And beach-glamour hasn't completely taken over yet. On a late-afternoon walk I noticed a goatherd tending his flock while only a couple of hundred yards away a rowdy group of Russian-speaking men headed into Skirts, a neon-emblazoned "gentleman's club."

Though the tourists flock to the beaches, many Greek Cypriots spend their weekends in the cooler Troodos Mountains to the west. The mountains are high enough to get occasional snow, which led to an architectural innovation for the churches. The melting snow would leak through the church domes, damaging the artwork inside. So wooden and tiled roofs were erected over the domes. The style is referred to as Mountain Byzantine.

At the tiny village of Trimilinkni, after we visited one such church, I asked our tour guide, Demetra, about her family's history on the island. Her family had lived in the Troodos, an area of scant resources. "My grandfather," she told me, "was the youngest of several children. On Sundays, a chunk of bread was doled out to each, their only food for the entire week, and he soon learned that his brothers would take it from him; they would find it even if he hid it.

"Finally, he asked his grandmother what to do. She told him to give it to her. She would then give him part of it each day, until the next Sunday when he would get his fresh piece. That way, his food for the week was kept safe."

Though there are still poor people on the republic side, that kind of extreme poverty is rare. In the five weeks I was on the island, I saw no one sleeping in doorways, no one begging, and, outside of partying tourists, only one obvious drunk.

But like in many cities of Europe and the United States, there are signs of exploitation of women from southeast Asia. Nightfall finds Asian prostitutes in heavy-traffic areas just inside the Venetian Walls. Just down the street from a Maronite Church in Nicosia's Old City is the office of a women's aid organization offering help to women lured to the island by promises of jobs.

Radiating out from the old-town areas (each city has its section, some defined by walls, others not), are the suburbs, the funny-looking lettering on the signs the only evident difference from those of, say, Phoenix, Arizona. But the prosperity and its new vacation mansions seem a bit tenuous given the island's periodic water shortages. In 2010 the island was struggling to recover from the previous two years when there was no measurable rainfall. Despite such problems, thirsty golf-course developments are being touted around the beach resorts.

The boom in the republic is not shared by the occupied side. Though the border-crossing section of Ledra Street seems on the surface to match its counterparts on the Greek side, the shops and restaurants end after a couple of blocks, replaced by abandoned, trash-filled buildings. Only a block or so from the restored caravanserai, I noticed an old man lying ill on dirty sheets just inside his front door, which opens onto the street. The harsh light of a bare bulb hanging from the ceiling made his plight visible to passers-by.

Recently, the Turkish government decided to allow residents of the occupied side to freely cross the Green Line for day jobs in the republic, a major concession. The official stance of the republic is that all islanders are entitled to Cypriot passports, but Turkey tells residents of the occupied side that they are citizens of the Turkish Republic of Northern Cyprus, a designation that realistically means they are people without a country.

The island's division infuses all conversations with visitors, despite attempts by businessmen such as Mustapha to downplay it. On the republic side, business owners are quick to correct references to the Turkish side: "you mean 'occupied side,'" I was told more than once.

In the Troodos, at another Mountain Byzantine church, the elderly caretaker insisted I photograph the graves of the Greek-speaking men who died fighting during the '74 invasion.

The church is in Fikardou, a small village that lost so many males during the conflict that the remaining residents abandoned it. It is now being restored as a World Heritage site.

Such reminders are everywhere on the island, underscoring the fact that though Cyprus is a respectable member of the European Union and a popular beach destination, it still depends on its strategic location for its political importance. Perhaps the most emblematic is the view from Cape Greco, on the eastern coast facing the Levant to the east and south. There, an elaborate British military listening post towers over a small, white-washed Orthodox church, providing "ears" during the periodic Mideastern upheavals, legacy of millennials-old conflict.

Egypt

As we prepared to board the Greek-based cruise ship at Limassol, the primary port of Cyprus, a dozen or so of the boat's crew, spiffy in their uniforms, lined up to greet us.

They quickly noticed that our group was primarily college-aged females and made inappropriate remarks to each other – in Arabic – all the while smiling at the girls. But thanks to one of our group's familiarity with their language, they were quickly called out. The hoots from the rest of our group left the would-be Lotharios red-faced – and nervously glancing at the ship's officers glaring at them from the deck.

Zaina Budayr's father is Lebanese, but after schooling in Geneva and meeting his future wife there, he had immigrated to the U.S. Zaina was born in New York City, where her father did his medical residency. Zaina's mother is a native of Sweden, and Zaina's childhood always included summer time in both Lebanon and Sweden. Her knowledge of the Arabic language and culture would come in handy during out four-week tenure in the Eastern Mediterranean.

We were rudely welcomed to Egypt's corruption before we officially entered the country at Port Said. The space between the gangplank and the immigration/customs shed is occupied by about a dozen vendors, tables set with their fake papyrus, guidebooks ("in English"), postcards, tote bags, pseudo-carved camels and pyramids and sphinxes. Obviously, they had reached some kind of "arrangement" with the officials so they could accost us before we had officially entered the country.

The gauntlet continues beyond security – in fact all the way to the tour bus waiting outside. The vendors are persistent, entreating us with their friendship, wanting to shake our hands. One member of the group has his hat removed by a tote salesman and placed in a bag that is then hung on his arm, all in one fluid motion. But a few well-chosen words from Zaina brought at least a modicum of relief from the constant attention.

The rampant corruption is one reason that extremist Islam has made inroads in Egypt, inroads that have prompted the government to establish a division of Tourism Police, providing armed escorts for all tourist buses that make the 150-mile trip between Port Said and Cairo.

Our Egyptian guide, Hanan, points out the government

concern as our three-bus convoy begins winding through Port Said, police cars and motorcycles ensuring that our path is clear in spite of rush-hour traffic. The government, she says, provides such services to show the world that Egypt is safe. Hanan, obviously, does not appreciate the irony of her statement.

We soon learn that the bus driver and Hanan, like the vendors, have their own hustles. The driver has cold drinks for sale; Hanan tells us about the cartouche of Pharoanic Egypt and then passes around a catalogue offering cartouches with the name of our choice embossed in Egyptian heiroglyphics.

As Hanan tells us about Egypt's ancient glory, we watch as the country's present reality unfolds along the highway.

There are conical pigeon-raising coops, irrigated fields of vegetables being worked by hand, rundown and seemingly abandoned mud-brick buildings, their occupation revealed by clothes fluttering on lines as they dry.

There are donkey carts, roadside stands filled with piles of melons and mangoes and other fruits and vegetables. Donkeys and goats are ever-present; occasionally there are horses, a couple of water buffalo. Mechanized farm equipment is rare – in the entire trip, we see maybe three tractors.

Everything is dust-covered, and everything says poverty.

We run close to the Suez Canal, passing the occasional looming ship, seeing the western edge of the Sinai desert across the waterway. At checkpoints, our escorts change. Sometimes it's Tourism Police, sometimes it's regular police, sometimes it's soldiers. All are armed with automatic rifles. The Tourism

Police have distinctive all-white uniforms; the soldiers dress in military camo. Their vehicles are small pickup trucks, they ride in the back facing our convoy with rifles at the ready. Their young ages and bored looks don't engender much confidence.

We pass donkey cart after donkey cart. We pass Vespa-style scooters, sometimes with children aboard. One female driver balances an infant between the handlebars. Another driver is accompanied by his veiled wife, riding side-saddle.

As we reach the industrialized outskirts of Cairo we notice each business is surrounded by a wall, most topped with razor-wire, many with guard towers attached.

Apartment complexes, vast in size, start to dominate. All seem unfinished, stopping after four or five stories, with rebar sticking from the roofs. Later Hanan tells us that is because the government doesn't tax buildings until they are finished; the builders never want to call a building finished.

We enter Heliopolis, a neighborhood of prosperity, with fancy hotels and mansions, side streets paved, a rarity, as we will discover. There is Shepheard's Hotel, the British-empire landmark, still in business. There is a Four Seasons, dominating one block. There is the American Embassy, secure behind thick, high walls and armed, alert-looking U.S. soldiers. At one intersection, an old lady in black, her feet bare, sits begging on the curb as BMWs, Mercedes, and Jaguars pass in front of her.

Heliopolis, Hanan tells us, is where President Mubarak resides with his family.

In Cairo, headed for the Egyptian Archeological Museum, home of its greatest treasures – and more hustle practitioners.

The museum is crowded with hordes of tourists, each supplied with a "whisperer" and accompanying headphones. The amplification devices are necessary as each guide is speaking to an individual group. Otherwise each tourist would be overwhelmed by a barrage of languages.

We hit only the highest of high spots: Rameses and King Tut. And then we're introduced to an archeologist friend of Hanan, who has DVDs for sale. Each contains more than 1,500 photos of the museum's treasures, and costs only 12 euros. Hanan's second hustle of the day.

We have our "Nile cruise" lunch, eating as the boat makes a large circle along the river. The food is mediocre, the music desultory. A belly-dancer then works her way through the crowd with a photographer accomplice taking pictures that will later be offered for sale to each subject.

Back on the bus for our next stop, the Giza pyramids and the Sphinx. And the serious gauntlet of camel jockeys, purveyors of everything imaginable, pickpockets and their child accomplices, and, perhaps most telling, a Tourism Policeman on the make.

To escape the camel jockeys, a couple of us climb the rocks off to one side of the pyramids. There, a uniformed officer beckons us to a spot for what he says is the best picture. Trusting no one at this point, we refuse to hand him our cameras so he can take the photo. Finally he gives up.

We move down the hill to the Sphinx, where we encounter more of the same, though the vendors here are mostly children. Here, Stephen encounters a child who claims to have picked up a euro belonging to him. But

Stephen has already been warned. The ploy is to discover in which pocket the mark keeps his money, making a pickpocket's job easier.

Zaina is besieged by another child, this one selling postcards. She begins talking to him in his native language, and he tells her that he is five years old and is tired. She gives him a $5 bill and tells him it is just for him, that he must not give it to anyone else. His smile is ear-to-ear as he is overwhelmed by the kindness of his "mark."

By now, everyone has had enough of Egypt. But we have one more stop, thanks to Hanan. A nearby papyrus museum has special deals for us. And the cartouche shop, where we can pick up whatever we ordered earlier, is upstairs.

As the buses sit outside, armed Tourism Police stand on the sidewalk at the front and back. It's good to know that we are well-protected even as the hustle continues inside the shop.

The ride back to our ship is quiet; we lose our driver and Hanan as they get off near Port Said after passing around an envelope for tips. There is one last run through the vendor gauntlet, and then we're safely on-board, everyone glad to see Egypt fading away in the rear-view mirror as we began our overnight sail back to Cyprus.

Like all cruise ships, the Filoxenia provides passengers with entertainment. There are floor shows coming and going featuring four female dancers. And when we arrive at Limossol, ready to disembark, we meet the dancers again – the ship is small enough that cast members have other duties and the dancers are assigned to see that everyone gets off the ship without incident.

But thick fog means we are stuck off the coast until it clears. So I spend a couple of hours in conversation with Alexandria and one of her fellow dancers. Alexandria speaks enough English so that we can carry on a reasonable conversation, her translations involving her friend as well. The four dancers, I am told, are from Odessa, and have all been trained in classic ballet. They have nothing good to say about their employer on the ship. And, thanks to exposure to American movies, especially Gene Kelly's

Transportation in Giza, camels to buses

classic musical "On the Town," dream of immigrating to New York. So we laugh as Alexandria and I come up with different ways to smuggle them into the U.S.

More recent developments – Vladimir Putin's brutal invasion of Ukraine in 2022 – make their return to Odessa problematic. I hope they either found a way into the U.S. or safe haven on Cyprus.

Opinions, Informed
& Otherwise

Frankie Carle to Loretta Lynn; Helen Humes to Flatt & Scruggs; baseball and its scribes; with brief musical appearances by Duke Ellington and Mother Maybelle, writer Sinclair Lewis, and baseballer Dock Ellis.

My first memories of music involve my mother and an Italian-American pianist and songsmith named Francis Nunzio Carlone. When I was a child, before my siblings came along, Mom played her piano, a well-seasoned upright, just about every day. Her favorite song was also well-seasoned, a tune by Carlone, who had anglicized his name to Frankie Carle. "Sunrise Serenade" had been released in 1938 when Mom was in her late teens.

I'm sure Mom had other favorites, too. But when she sat down at the piano she always began with the serenade. And the melody was memorable enough that it stuck in my toddler brain.

My own efforts at playing music were not successful. I persevered through a year or so of saxophone lessons only because I was enamored of the teacher's teen-aged daughter and her curly red tresses.

But I was an interested listener, catching the early-TV show "Your Hit Parade" often enough to know that Frank Sinatra and Peggy Lee and Benny Goodman and Glenn Miller were important – like Carle, their names were soon associated with tunes in my mental catalog.

Then came Elvis Presley, whose hits sent me looking for his influences – Black blues artists like Arthur Crudup and Elmore James. Elvis was available everywhere, but recordings and appearances by his Black antecedents were more difficult to find. Other white musicians who were covering the styles of Black artists – Doc Pomus's "Lonely Avenue" and several of the songs penned by Leiber and Stoller for example – were easier to locate and ended up in my collection of 45 records.

Then I discovered Ray Charles. The first concert I attended was Ray Charles and his big band. A year or so later, when he brought the group back to Knoxville, I was seated first-row balcony so I could get a good view of the band and Ray as he moved back and forth from saxophone to piano to organ.

Charles' gospel-influenced approach involving top-shelf musicians and horn-heavy arrangements was soon dominating my record collection, now featuring LPs rather than 45s. From there, I was soon listening to jazz, notably the saxophone work of Cannonball Adderley and Stanley Turrentine.

In 1965 I began working part-time at *The Knoxville Journal* while attending the University of Tennessee, and it did not take me long to convince my bosses that I should write about popular music for *Journal* readers. Now I was a listener with a forum. Never mind that I did not know what I was talking about – none of my bosses knew enough about music to realize my ignorance, or even cared enough to read what I was producing. They only knew that they were getting extra work from me and it wasn't costing the *Journal* any money.

When Duke Ellington agreed to play at Knoxville's Cherokee Country Club in 1967, it was with the caveat that the band would also play at a venue that was open to all. So two shows – early and late – were scheduled at the Senators' Club, a venue with a democratic approach.

My *Journal* cohort Pat Fields was assigned to cover the early show, but she pushed for the bosses to allow me to attend the second so there would be no surprises that she would need for her story. So I heard the band from a front-row seat and, post-show, had brief conversations with Ellington, Johnny Hodges, Paul Gonsalves and other members of the band.

But I was writing about the more typical music being played around Knoxville during that era, which thanks to the built-in audience provided by UT students was rock 'n' roll. I like to think that I introduced the staid readership of the *Journal* to the raucous pleasures of rock 'n' roll. In addition to many other acts, I covered a '60s Bob Dylan show when he first began touring with the musicians that later became The Band, and I was present when the Rolling Stones played Knoxville on their 1972 U.S. tour.

My interests encompassed other arts as well as music. By the first grade of school I was taking advantage of the public library, checking out the maximum six books every week, biographies and other non-fiction. And by the time I had finished high school, I was a dedicated movie buff.

As I moved around to different cities and different journalism tasks, I seized every opportunity to explore the arts. Over the decades, besides music and movies, I have also written about drama and visual art. As an editor, I was in the position of producing and directing photo shoots involving fashion, too.

When a dancer I knew in Louisville choreographed a number to Bonnie Raitt's version of a Randy Newman song, I assigned a story about it, and later maneuvered myself into photographing a program involving ballet lessons given by a pair of renowned masters of the art.

There was even a thankfully brief turn at writing about men's fashion while I was at *The Atlanta Journal-Constitution*. On the outs with the powers that be, I was given assignments involving trends in men's clothing – after I turned in a couple of stories, apparently the decision was made that I had been punished enough and I was relieved of those duties.

My love of books, combined with my East Tennessee roots, led to my excerpting Cormac McCarthy's "Blood Meridian" when I was at *The Dallas Times Herald*, long before McCarthy's work was known outside of academic circles.

While in Dallas, I volunteered to review music even though my primary job was assigning and editing work for the Sunday magazine. For the music reviews, I used a pseudonym, which eventually led to a problem. My alter ego garnered interest from one of the Houston newspaper editors who was looking for a new popular-music scribe. I decided I'd stick to my editing job and abandoned the pseudonymous alter ego, though he still lives on as a joke among my friends.

So this section involves examples of opinion writing, one for *The Louisville Times* involving the magic of jazz singer Helen Humes, another on the mastery of bluegrass legends Flatt and Scruggs for *The New York Times*, and the third an op-ed piece for *The Boston Globe* exploring the intersection of sports and literature.

Helen Humes

As popular music was going through major changes in the 1950s and 1960s, there was renewed interest in the aging innovators from the 1920s and 1930s. Blues works by Robert Johnson and Elmore James and Son House were being rediscovered as were jazz artists such as Lonnie Johnson and Charlie Christian. Helen Humes, a Louisville native who had been featured in Count Basie's band in the 1940s, was one of the "forgotten" Black entertainers who was rediscovered.

After years of touring and working in New York City and on the West Coast, she had returned to her hometown in the mid 1950s to take care of her mother. She had quit singing professionally, gotten rid of her record collection, and eventually took a job at an ammunition factory. But writer Stanley Dance persuaded her to return to music in the late 1960s, and she was soon a regular on the stage at Barney Josephson's Cookery nightclub in Manhattan.

In 1979 she returned to Louisville with accompanist Ellis Larkins for a three-day gig at a downtown nightclub.

I was not familiar with her work, but after reading a couple of reviews I made sure to be there – and ended up attending two of the performances as she demonstrated why she is generally ranked in the top tier of jazz and blues singers.

During one break she stopped by the table occupied by me and several friends, proving to be as gracious as she was gifted.

In slightly different form, here is my *Louisville Times* take:

There are many things that stand out in a performance by Miss Humes. The clarity of her little-girl voice. The exuberance of her delivery. The wide range of her song selection. The way she appears to be able to do anything with her voice. And the seeming ease with which she does it.

But the thing that sticks most is the sense of fun she exudes – she's having an infectious good time.

Miss Humes was undeterred by a throat problem and a Louisville-club mainstay – rude members of the audience. She did everything she tried with her voice, and she tried everything – clipping her words perfunctorily, holding notes, "rasping" on blues numbers. And always with natural ease, as if she was just noodling around for fun.

She sang "Lover Man," the song made famous by Billie Holiday, whom Miss Humes replaced in Count Basie's band in the 1940s. She sang Bessie Smith's classic "Nobody Knows You When You're Down and Out;" Fats Waller's "Viper," one of the more famous "reefer" numbers; the witty "He May Be Your Man," and "Old Men."

Part of Miss Humes' charm is the little-girl voice delivering such lines as "He may be your man, but he comes to see me sometimes," and comparing the advantages of loving an old man and a young one.

She worked inside each song, here pushing it to its limits, there sliding it back down, slowing it for soulful impact. Whatever emotion she sought to evoke she simply moved the song around to the perfect point for that feel, demonstrating such musical mastery that no matter the tune, at song's end, she owned it.

Flatt & Scruggs

Growing up in Knoxville during the fertile rock 'n' roll years, I did not pay much attention to country music, which dominated southern radio during that era. It was only later, when my musical tastes had matured, that I noticed the mastery of fellow southern Appalachians Chet Atkins, Roy Acuff, Dolly Parton and others.

When I was at *The Miami Herald*, working as a copy editor, I reviewed a concert by Loretta Lynn and Conway Twitty – the first country act that I attended. I was sent across Biscayne Bay to the Miami Beach venue because the arts editor had decided that the show should be covered.

As far as I know it was the first time that *The Herald* had ever "stooped" to reporting on country music. Asking around the newsroom, the editors were told that Wohlwend, the new guy on the national desk, was from Tennessee, so he probably knew country music. I didn't tell them any different, though I did not own any country records at the time. I was dispatched to the show. And a couple of hours later I headed back across the bay a convinced fan of Loretta Lynn (Twitty? Not so much).

My review was published the next day, and I had to listen to my "sophisticated" cohorts make fun of me for calling Loretta Lynn a "downhome diva."

Later, in Louisville in the late 1970s, my record collection had grown to include work by Flatt & Scruggs, Vassar Clements, Waylon Jennings, the Nitty Gritty Dirt Band. And I was regularly attending shows by Louisville's own New Grass Revival and other innovating "country" acts.

In 2007, tapes of early 1960s television performances by Lester Flatt and Earl Scruggs and their group, the Foggy Mountain Boys, were discovered, brought back to reproducible condition and released. *The New York Times* asked me to write about the first four episodes that were made available. Here's the result:

During a television performance in 1961 the bluegrass guitarist and singer Lester Flatt introduced his partner, the banjoist Earl Scruggs, with the line "He kind of likes to show off anyway, pickin' the hot stuff."

Scruggs didn't waste time bantering back. He immediately began showing off, launching into a fiery-fingered version of "Georgia Buck."

The exchange was typical of the two men, who were instrumental in introducing bluegrass music to a wide audience, and it's featured on a pair of new releases from Shanachie Entertainment in partnership with the Country Music Hall of Fame and Museum. Each of the two DVDs comprises a pair of episodes of the 30-minute "Flatt & Scruggs Grand Ole Opry Show." The discs are an overdue reminder of the important role the duo played in building a national audience for this American music.

Bluegrass, first popularized in the 1930s and '40s by Flatt & Scruggs's mentor, Bill Monroe, has always appealed to musicians because its fast and dexterous finger work demands concentration from its practitioners. Scruggs pioneered a three-fingered technique that is now a mainstay of the music, known as Scruggs-style picking.

While Flatt did the singing and most of the talking, Scruggs preferred to let his playing speak, as the pair and their band, the Foggy Mountain Boys, worked their way through tunes that were almost always fast paced, whether freshly composed or derived from the traditional Scots-Irish folk songs popular in their native southern Appalachia.

The episodes featured on the DVDs, three from 1961 and one from 1962, are well chosen, with classic tunes and a guest appearance by Mother Maybelle Carter, a member of the fabled Carter Family. Another regular guest, Hylo Brown, displays his impressive falsetto with a two-part "John Henry."

Other standouts include Mother Maybelle's version of "Wildwood Flower" and the instrumental "Liberty Dance" on autoharp, and the Foggy Mountain Boys' take on the haunting "Jimmie Brown the Newsboy." Bluegrass standards like "Durham's Bull" and "Shortnin' Bread" are also featured.

The production has a relaxed, back-porch feel. The set is simple, cigarette packs are visible in shirt pockets, and the commercials include recipes.

Song dedications are quickly read from the back of an envelope, the cornball jokes are mercifully brief, and at one point Flatt tells any potential promoters in the audience that the band has several open dates on a coming tour, providing the address to write for terms. But the nonmusical segments go quickly, as if the pace of the picking has insinuated itself into the entire show. The musicians swiftly dispense with the talking to get back to the fun stuff.

Typically each show features two tunes, a commercial and then two more songs before Flatt introduces what he called a "sacred" tune. Then there is another ad, more picking and singing, and another hymn before the final two songs.

Often a guest provides one or two tunes per segment. Scruggs mostly works with the five-string banjo, though sometimes he switches to guitar. Flatt was an excellent guitarist, but is better known for his nasal, classic-country singing and for being the quick-with-a-laugh voice of the pair.

The show, produced in Nashville, was featured on stations through the Southeast from 1955 until 1969. Tapes of the show were believed destroyed until they were discovered in a home garage in 1989.

In the late 1950s, when popular music began expanding in styles and audience thanks to long-playing albums and television, Flatt & Scruggs, partners since the mid-1940s, were poised to take advantage. They soon became favorites of the college-based folk revival of the early 1960s.

By the fall of 1962 the pair and their band were enough of a fixture that CBS enlisted them to provide theme music for

the network television comedy "The Beverly Hillbillies." The exposure brought national fame, and in 1967 their "Foggy Mountain Breakdown" was used in the movie "Bonnie and Clyde." "Breakdown" had long been the group's signature, and the Hall of Fame release wisely includes a noteworthy version from the August 1961 episode.

The fiddler Paul Warren's bow makes his instrument sing before Josh Graves counters with a dobro solo. But it is Scruggs who drives the tune, flying fingers demonstrating just why three-finger picking is still called Scruggs-style. And why Flatt & Scruggs are synonymous with this distinctive Appalachian art form.

Baseball and Its Poetic Chroniclers

In late winter, 1994, as newspaper sports sections began publishing baseball spring-training stories, I got the idea to look at the contrast between the professionals involved in the game and the writers who annually elevated the game to heights enjoyed by no other sport. They approached the game as if it were a religion, ignoring the players' peccadillos involving alcohol, hallucinogenic drugs, money-grubbing, and cheating as extreme as throwing games for the benefit of bettors.

I pitched the idea to editor Michael Larkin of *The Boston Globe*. Here's the result, updated with more recent transgressions. The column ran in Focus, the Sunday paper's opinion section, under the headline "Prose Strikes Out."

The scribes, stimulated by the sunshine of Florida or Arizona, have filed their first spring-training stories, thrown out their first cliches of the season.

And as sure as the hopeful reports will continue from Fort Myers or Scottsdale, as sure as the Houston Astros — individually and en masse — will do something immoral, baseball's great myth, its greatest cliche, will again be perpetrated.

The literary lions will send back their musings about the boys of summer, about baseball as metaphor, about baseball as life itself. And once again, the seemingly intelligent among the fans will embrace their words, smiling at sentences praising baseball as the intellectual sport, as the pastime for thinkers.

A W.P. Kinsella will print it and they will come. A John Updike will describe a "lyric little bandbox of a ballpark" and they will look at each other and nod knowingly. A David Halberstam will windily proclaim that the game will seem "more than almost anything else … to symbolize normalcy."

The game will transcend other, less intellectual sports and become The Game. "Grace" and "elegance" and "ballet" will appear in the same sentences as "double play" and "shoe-top catch." Laboriously, a George Will sentence will rhapsodize about the Craft and what it requires in watching. "Being a serious baseball fan, meaning an informed and attentive and observant fan … is doing something that makes demands on the mind of the doer," he argued in "Men at Work."

But as the exhibition games begin, the observant fan will note overweight human caricatures grotesquely stuffed into stretched knit uniforms. Patient, he will watch as they make obscene adjustments. Curious, he will wonder at what they are hiding under their neck-beards. Attentive, he will notice the oozing tobacco spittle and how it forms a brown accent line on the chin, as effective as face paint in establishing a clown.

He will stand and yell when these comic characters rush at each other, arms flailing, and fall to the ground in imitation of professional wrestling. He will shake his head when managers and umpires stand belly to belly, heads wagging, mouths moving.

After the game, maybe these grotesques will grace the fan with lighted firecrackers, if there's still time after they've sprayed bleach at sportswriters or invectives at their teammates. The more intelligent of those fans will be safe at home when the clowns hold the bar-brawl ritual that often enough closes their day's activity.

And the writers will continue their homage. Baseball is, Will continued, "a game that rewards, and thus elicits, a remarkable level of intelligence from those who compete."

And how about the intelligence of those who manage and own? George Steinbrenner and Pete Rose? Or going back to earlier periods, Billy Martin, Horace Stoneman, Bill Veeck and Charles Finley?

In 1983, only a year after a cocaine scandal in the Kansas City Royals clubhouse, the late Sparky Anderson, pennant-winning manager and revered baseball mind, profoundly observed, "In the old days, 24 of the 25 guys on every team were drunk. Today, nobody hardly drinks anymore, and very few take drugs."

The late Warren Giles was asked about drug use when he was president of the National League in 1969. "It has never come up, and I don't think it ever will," he proclaimed. Over in the American League, spokesman Bob Holbrook agreed: "Baseball players don't use those types of things."

The players, with their "remarkable level of intelligence," were finding higher truth in other ways. Before steroids became the sluggers' drug of choice, there were other chemical diversions.

The late Dock Ellis, who partied with Jimi Hendrix and pitched a no-hitter for the Pirates under the influence of LSD in 1970, told an interviewer after his career was finished: "I was using everything, I mean everything. For about eight or nine years, I was an addict."

Bob Uecker, once a journeyman catcher and later a beer pitchman, found his high the old-fashioned way. "Anybody can play sober," he once said. "I liked to get out there and play liquored up."

When steroids became popular, when home runs not only had to leave the park, but had to do it spectacularly, the Game's fans witnessed hero after hero eventually confessing their transgressions.

Still, Thomas Boswell, the retired Washington Post sportswriter, could muse on The Game's "sense of moderation — of both physical and emotional temperance."

And novelist George V. Higgins could write, "Baseball is to our everyday experience what poetry often is to common speech — a slightly elevated and concentrated form."

Maybe the writers view the display on the field (and off) as the ancient Romans did their spectator "games": aristocracy enjoying the skills — and follies — of the plebeian class.

Or maybe it isn't really The Game itself, but the musings themselves, as the late William Zinsser wisely noted in his book, "Spring Training": "Writing about baseball seemed to be some kind of validating rite for the American male."

Or maybe it is simple guilt. A baseball game consumes several hours, time that could be spent on the Great American Novel, on an insightful political treatise, or a profound philosophical tome. The game must be elevated to The Game to atone for wasted time. That's the way Sinclair Lewis saw it. Cocking a cynical eye on the lower-case game in his novel "Babbitt," Lewis wrote: "But the game was a custom of his clan and it gave outlet for the homicidal and sides-taking instincts which Babbitt called 'patriotism' and 'love of sport.' No sense a man's working his fool head off. I'm going to the game three days a week."

Characters & Contention

The relationship between editors and writers is complicated. In my peripatetic career I have dealt with a variety of bosses: a handful were ego-driven tyrants; a couple were talented but hard-drinking personalities; and there were a few who were competent, even-tempered professionals, pleasant and reliable. The same list of characteristics works for the writers who I have guided through assignments.

Each personality requires a unique approach on my part. If the end product is worth the effort, I put up with the problems; if it is not I only work with them when I have no choice. The accounts that follow are of a few exemplary writers – each of whom I enjoyed working with.

When I agreed to move to *The Dallas Times Herald* for a Sunday magazine editing position in 1980, the powers that be had already assigned stories to several of the newspaper's best writers for the new publication, to be called *Westward*. During my first days on the job, I was introduced to two of them.

The newspaper had assigned an empty office to *Westward* and I was settling into my desk when Jim Henderson walked in. I was struck by his large frame and his sartorial choices – a business suit accessorized with well-worn cowboy boots. We talked about the story he was working on and then he stopped at the door before returning to his newsroom desk.

"By the way," he said, "I should warn you that one of the other reporters, Jim Schutze, is also working on a *Westward* piece, and you should know that he's not very good – you'll have to push him on the reporting and you'll probably have to rewrite him." Before I could respond, Henderson was out the door and gone.

That was odd, I thought. But my more pressing problem concerned the primitive word-processing computer that was sitting on my desk, so I went back to figuring it out.

In a few minutes another staffer walked in. He sported a carefully trimmed beard and was wearing a three-piece suit properly accessorized with wing-tipped dress shoes. He introduced himself as Jim Schutze and told me about the *Westward* story he was working on. We commiserated about the word-processing problem and then he got up to take his leave.

When he got to the door, he turned around. "By the way," he said, "one of my newsroom cohorts is also working on a story for you. He can be a real problem – sloppy reporting and he can't write. His name is Jim Henderson and you'll need to be careful with his stories."

I realized then that I had been had.

As it turned out, both Henderson and Schutze produced

excellent work, and were key to *Westward's* success. And, I later learned, Henderson only wore cowboy boots because the newspaper's editor, Ken Johnson, did not want staffers to look like cowboys. When Henderson saw Johnson approaching, he would lean back in his chair and place his boot-clad feet on his desk just so Johnson would notice.

Other *Times Herald* characters were soon making frequent visits to the *Westward* office. Because we were the Sunday magazine, we offered reporters something they could not get on their regular beat – space for longer stories and the chance to approach a subject from a different viewpoint. Photographers could use color film and expect layouts with multiple photos. Our art director, James Noel Smith, possessed a great eye and his opinions were valued. Our office was a popular spot.

The newsroom veterans would soon be joined by Richard Boeth, a diminutive New Yorker who possessed great talent and many personal demons. Boeth shared a common reporters' trait: a disdain for authority. He was responsible for several nose-thumbing stories, a couple of which are related below.

I met Boeth (pronounced Booth) when complex circumstances brought him to Denton, Texas in 1980. A native of England, he had been a top juniors tennis player, had graduated from Princeton University and, in his own telling, had become a senior writer at *Time* magazine "and an alcoholic" by the time he was 25.

My immediate boss, Kerry Slagle, a friend from my days at *The Miami Herald* in the early 1970s, had known Boeth in New York when their paths crossed in the hallways of *Newsweek* magazine. Slagle had recognized Boeth's writing gifts, and he knew that he had recently moved to Denton. In his early 40s, Boeth had been diagnosed with a rare cancer and had undergone several rough weeks of treatment in a Manhattan facility. There, he became friends with one of his caregivers, a nurse who was a Denton native. After the cancer went into remission, he followed her to Texas.

Slagle invited Boeth to a Dallas lunch to discuss producing free-lance stories for us. Before the meeting, he gave me several Boeth clips – and provided the details of his drinking history as well as his successful defeat of that particular demon.

Our guest arrived in an irritable mood. He had, he explained, recently applied for a job at one of Denton's major employers, a vast Peterbilt truck-building facility. He was invited for an interview, but, he told us, "they did not want me for the assembly line, which is what I was interested in." After looking at his background, "they wanted to talk about something to do with company communications; I wanted work that was mindless."

After a few minutes of free-lance talk, Boeth looked at Slagle and said, "Why don't you hire me as your staff writer, full-time?"

Surprised, Slagle answered, "Well, that's an idea we hadn't thought of. Let me see what I can do." A few days later, Slagle managed to convince the *Times Herald* brass that *Westward* should have a full-time staff writer — and Boeth had moved into our office. He set up his desk alongside mine on the back wall. From there, we had clear sight-paths to both doors as well as the space behind Slagle's post — important because we could see him when he was napping underneath his desk to escape the sight of passing executives.

When the managing editor or the photography director came looking for Slagle, we knew after a quick glance that he was not to be disturbed. "He was here just a minute ago," one of us would explain. "He's probably out in the newsroom," art director James Noel might add. That way we stayed on Slagle's good side. Boeth's years of experience in Manhattan news hubs meant he quickly realized the wisdom of our office layout, and with a wry grin announced his approval: "And we have blackmail material over Slagle," he pointed out.

Our office had other advantages, too. It had formerly been the executive dining room, which meant it was just across the hall from the company cafeteria, but still separate from the main newsroom and the features department. We could reach the elevators (both front and rear) without being seen by the brass or nosy co-workers.

And that added to our attraction as an escape from the newsroom. That also meant that another of Boeth's attributes quickly became evident — he had an eye for the females, frequent visitors to our space on their way to and from the cafeteria.

And, since my desk was close to his, he started asking me about the availability of the ones who caught his eye. In the process, he confessed that his nurse/girlfriend in Denton had encouraged him to find another place to live, suggesting that it should be at least as far away as Dallas, which was about 50 miles south of her home.

Pressed, he told me that he had been married "three and a half times." The "half," he said, represented his first and third wife, whom he had divorced to marry the second, then re-married when the second one kicked him out.

I learned other tidbits of his past, too. His roommate at

Princeton had been Wayne Rogers, then starring as Trapper John on the popular television series, "M*A*S*H". Another Princeton buddy was John McPhee, one of the leading practitioners of what had become known as "new journalism." During a news-magazine stint in Chicago, one of his drinking buddies had been Frederick Exley, who later wrote the acclaimed "novel" of his life, "A Fan's Notes." Their friendship, Boeth said, deteriorated into an alcoholic free-for-all. "State Street," Boeth said, citing the song lyric, "was only a great street when we were drunk."

Boeth's restless energy quickly paid dividends for *Westward*. He knew that we saw our coverage area as the entire Southwest, and he paid attention to the latest news from what we saw as our readership range, pitching story ideas that interested him.

And Slagle was adept at keeping him happy even when it meant slipping in assignments that he knew the brass would neither understand nor approve. So Boeth would turn in a brilliantly reported and written story that was conventional – taking the regularly scheduled gambling bus to Louisiana Downs to portray the punters as they wagered on the ponies, for example. He followed that story with a trip to Oklahoma for a Germaine Greer interview/essay about her new visiting professorship at the University of Tulsa.

The Greer story pitted two smart, middle-aged writers who were both new enough to the American west to find it fascinatingly foreign. And given their common interest in the subject the pair ended up obsessing on a favorite topic – human sexuality.

The story ended with Greer's confession that "what I like best about men is how much they like me. A stiff dick goes a long way toward convincing me that everything's okay." We ran the story with Ms. Greer's comment as "stiff d- - -". Slagle was reasonably sure that given the subject matter – a leading feminist author – the story would probably not be read by the newspaper brass. He was correct; the only comments we heard were chuckles from like-minded newsroom cohorts.

But Boeth's most personal story confronted his alcohol demon. In a cover story titled "On Drunks" he combined alcohol's history, its relationship with psychiatry, and his own experiences into a definitive account. The story and artwork were national-award winners.

Another Boethian foray into sex came in an essay. We had begun a column called Westwords, and Boeth wanted to write a fictionalized "personal" account. He fashioned an alter ego that he called Paul Wells, a "melancholy free-lance intellectual". Wells, according to his creator, had by age 35 "been through seven live-in arrangements, three marriages (one open, one closed and one sneaky) and a brief stint as a barker at a freak show."

The author and Paul Wells then debated the relationships between male and female for several hundred words before ending the essay thusly: "What the hell, sex has been driving us all crazy for 5,000 years and it sure ain't going to stop now."

In the summer of 1981, Boeth's cancer returned. After considering his options, he decided he was not going to repeat the treatments he had survived earlier. He worked long as he could, then took to his apartment. Caregivers and friends regularly checked in on him. During one of my last visits, he handed me a copy of *The Atlantic* magazine from the late 1960s and told me to read a particular piece.

The article was built around the several months he had lived in the Mississippi Delta with his girlfriend at the time. "She was a Mississippi native, daughter of a long-time plantation-holding family," he said. "My knowledge of the Delta, of course, was based on the civil-rights movement and the press it was generating. The editors of *The Atlantic* wanted my take on the area given its history."

The story, not surprisingly, was brilliant – clear-eyed insights, beautifully told. When I finished it, I said as much to its author.

"Yeah," he said, "sometimes I wonder what I could have done if I hadn't of been a slave to my cock all my life."

He died a month or so later, aged 48.

Stanley Booth

When I moved to Atlanta in 1984 to become editor of *Atlanta Weekly*, the Sunday magazine of *The Atlanta Journal-Constitution*, I soon was working with another notable writer named Booth. Stanley Booth used the conventional spelling of his name, but there was nothing conventional about its bearer, as my next-door neighbor discovered early one morning as she watched a white limousine pull into my driveway.

My condo was on the corner of two short dead-end streets – limos were not common. As she watched, the chauffeur exited to help a male occupant out of the vehicle's rear seat, guiding him to the front door of my house. Then the driver got back into his vehicle and the car slowly left the subdivision.

Knowing that I frequently departed for my job at about 7 a.m., my curious neighbor correctly assumed that I was already at work. She phoned to excitedly report what she had seen, adding that there was another person in the limo and that it appeared to be a female, but she couldn't be sure as the vehicle's windows were dark.

"That would be Stanley Booth arriving after an all-nighter," I reassured her. "I noticed he was not back when I left this morning. Glad to see that he made it. And thanks for keeping an eye on my place." Asked who the other occupant was, I laughed. "With Stanley, it could be anyone," I said.

I had left Stanley the previous evening shortly before midnight at a fancy apartment in Smyrna because I needed to be at work early the next morning. "Don't worry," he had told me. "I'll manage to get back to your place." And Memphis soul diva Carla Thomas was more than happy to see him home.

Stanley was in Atlanta to cover a package-artist concert featuring acts from Memphis's Stax label. Carla was one of the headliners, along with her father, Rufus Thomas. Others included Sam & Dave, Eddie Floyd, and Luther Ingram. I had joined him backstage at the show the night before. And we had then joined the headliners at their post-performance party at the home of one of the show's producers. Stanley and I were, as Rufus laughingly pointed out, the only "cracker peckerwoods" present.

Stanley became friends with the Thomas family when he was college-age and living in Memphis. He had charmed his way into recording sessions until he was on a first-name basis with Jim Dickinson and other stalwarts of the Memphis Sound. When Otis Redding put the finishing touches on "Sitting on the Dock of the Bay", Stanley was seated a few feet away.

In fact, Stanley Booth, though unknown to my neighbors, occupies a legendary position in music journalism, conversant with artists ranging from Furry Lewis to Keith Richards to Johnny Mercer. His carefully constructed reports and opinions on music and its importance to the creative turmoil of the '60s graced the pages of *Esquire, Rolling Stone* and *Playboy* magazines.

I had been introduced to Stanley shortly after I moved to Atlanta from Kansas City in 1984. I had read his remarkable account of the Rolling Stones' 1969 tour of the U.S., "The True Adventures of the Rolling Stones", which was first published in the U.S. with the title "Dance with the Devil." After discovering that he was living in Brunswick, Georgia, I decided that he was a likely subject for an *Atlanta Weekly* profile.

One of my missions as editor was to liven the pages of the staid publication – in Stanley Booth, we could focus on sex, drugs, and rock 'n' roll with one brilliant and erudite native of south Georgia's piney woods. After contacting Stanley, I found the perfect writer to send to Brunswick. Tom Gray was an Atlanta musician, keyboardist and vocalist for The Brains, a New Wave group accomplished enough to headline festivals throughout the eastern U.S. and in Europe. Tom spent several days with Stanley – "talking every night until we ran out of wine," he told me.

The piece ran as a cover story, and, thanks to Tom Gray, our publication was soon being talked about by Atlanta's music scenesters. And Stanley and I were regularly engaged in phone conversations, discussing story ideas. Soon, he was producing articles for a column that I had created. "Southwords" was designed to attract the region's best writers by offering an open forum.

Stanley soon became a regular at my house, stopping in on forays to and from New York City and London, and, later, making my spare bedroom his headquarters when on assignment.

Stanley easily made himself at home, establishing a good relationship with Spot, my cat, and discovering obscure blues renditions buried in my record collection. A Piney Brown tune, "Whispering Blues," was a favorite – Stanley liked to quote a recurring line from the song: "Let me go home, Whiskey."

In addition, I was learning more about Stanley. He had a daughter by his first wife. But he was now single again and was living in Brunswick to be close to his parents and to his daughter, who lived with them. And, like my Dallas friend, Dick Boeth, his first wife was also his third after a divorce and re-marriage.

I had quickly noticed that Stanley possessed a remarkable memory. A phone call from Brunswick would frequently take up an hour or so, then I would not hear anything from him for a couple of months. But when I would pick up the ringing phone, he would immediately continue where our previous conversation had ended.

The conversations might be about his days in Memphis, hanging out with bluesman Furry Lewis, sitting in at Stax sessions, or visiting music entrepreneur Dewey Phillips. He told me about his own experience with Elvis Presley's physician, George C. Nichopoulos – Dr. Nick. "He saved me from a painkiller addiction," Stanley said. The drugs were prescribed after a fall in the north-Georgia mountains that had "nearly killed me," he explained. And he told of Memphis bar crawls with photographer

William Eggleston – including one "ill-advised" drug-fueled foray into Mexico.

In Stanley's telling, he had chosen his career path at about age 8 when he decided he was going to be a writer. After an education along normal paths, in Macon, Memphis and New Orleans, his work began appearing in national publications. He became one of the premier chroniclers and champions of Black contributions to American music.

Dr. Nick's success did not mean Stanley had given up all medications. To my surprise and consternation, one of his guests at my place was a bearded, 250-pound marijuana dealer. And after one of Stanley's visits I discovered that nothing remained of my muscle-relaxant prescription (compliments of the dentist who had pulled my wisdom teeth) except the empty bottle.

Another marijuana quest on one of his Atlanta visits led Stanley to a hair-raising confrontation. He had borrowed his mother's Chevrolet station wagon. When he drove it to a drive-up teller machine to withdraw money for a weed purchase, a neophyte robber confronted him with a pistol.

Stanley's answer was to turn and quickly run toward a doughnut shop a block away, making sure that the station wagon was between him and the perp's pistol. After he told me about his escape, we went back the next day and re-enacted the scene from the robber's viewpoint. The accompanying photos depict Stanley's quick thinking.

After one of Stanley's trips to London he called with a question about my Ampex reel-to-reel tape player. He remembered that it featured more than one speed. "Keith loaned me the original tapes that the Maysles brothers made at Altamont and Madison Square Garden," he said. "And I need to copy them from the high speed at which they were recorded to a slower speed so that I can play them." The Keith in question was Richards, and the Maysles were Albert and David, charged with making the official documentary of the 1969 Rolling Stones' tour.

My machine was not capable of the higher speed, but I knew someone who had more professional equipment. Soon, I was in possession of the Maysles tapes and they had been copied to reel-to-reel tape that my Ampex could handle, and then on to cassettes. Stanley got his copies, but, perhaps considering his habits and sometime companions, he opted to leave the originals with me. So I added them to my collection of homemade-tapes.

More than two years later, I got a call from Stanley. "I'm headed to London and have to get the tapes back to Keith," he said. "Can you meet me at Hartsfield?" I carefully packaged them, sealed them into a box and took them to the airport on the specified date. A couple of days later, the tapes were back in Keith's hands. And I had a clearer understanding of how bootleg music is continually being discovered.

Shortly before I decided to leave Atlanta, I assigned Stanley to cover the New Orleans Jazz Festival, the annual two-weekend music bacchanalia. He suggested that Eggleston accompany him to provide photos. Though I was sure that such a combination would probably lead to great coverage, I also understood that it would probably also generate headaches (if not bail money).

But I agreed to it, reasoning that since the *Journal-Constitution* was phasing out *Atlanta Weekly*, I wanted it to go out on top. The bosses were not paying much attention to what I was publishing – if they noticed my extravagance at all, I would already be gone. Stanley delivered on his part, but Eggleston never made it to the festival. "He had to get a girlfriend out of the institution where her family had committed her," Stanley explained.

Not long afterward, Stanley called with an unusual query. "I need to find one of those chenille bedspreads with the peacock design," he said. "Do you know where I can get one?"

His request was on the behalf of "this elderly Black lady that I've become friends with," he explained. He had noticed the woman carrying a bag of groceries on a two-lane highway in south Georgia and had offered her a ride.

"She lived in an old cabin down this dirt road," he said. "I ended up sitting on her porch talking about her life until it got dark."

He had begun periodically checking in on her, taking her to get groceries and generally making sure she was okay.

"She got to talking about the chenille bedspread she used

to have, so I thought I would see if I could find her one," he added. Her story, he didn't need to add, helped him keep his own travails in perspective.

The last time I saw Stanley was in 2014 when he was living in Memphis again, where he had moved after his most-recent wife had died unexpectedly. By then I had returned to East Tennessee and was now living a few miles from my boyhood home in Knoxville. Stanley was going to be in Atlanta to give a reading at Georgia State University. I arranged to pick him up the next day for lunch at a popular south Atlanta meat-and-three. Our mutual friend Tom Junod would join us.

Stanley was not in his usual upbeat mood. On the drive to the café, it was obvious that he was grieving over the loss of his wife, his mood exasperated by the pair's last months. "We were basically homeless," he said, "sleeping on the couches of friends." But he was dapper, as always, sporting a new look. He had swapped his Seville Row threads for fringed-and-beaded native-American duds.

At one point, as Stanley recounted the last months of his wife, he was asked how many times he had been married. "I've lost count," he answered with a shrug that made it clear that marital status was now off-the-table.

To change the subject, I reminded him of the stories he had told me of the elderly Black woman he had befriended a year or so earlier and asked about the peacock bedspread.

"I couldn't find her one," he said. "Then I discovered that she had passed. I guess that she, too, like the chenille, had just worn out."

William Hedgepeth

I first came in contact with the work of Atlanta writer Bill Hedgepeth when I was living in Louisville in the late 1970s when I discovered one of his best-known projects.

"The Hog Book" was a compendium of everything porcine, fact-driven but presented in a patently flamboyant way. As the newly named book columnist of *The Louisville Times* in 1978, I received a review copy of the oversized volume. Since the book was from a respected New York publisher and the cover featured a fanciful take-off on the Lady Godiva myth – the golden-tressed heroine was riding a pink pig – I quickly decided it needed my attention.

A quick run-through revealed more fanciful drawings by the cover artist, John Findley, and arresting pictures by Atlanta photographer Al Clayton. One of Clayton's shots featured a resting hog in front of a sheltering barn, staring at the camera. The caption was "Alert hog guarding a tractor". Chapter headings included "Swine in Art, Sport, and Show Biz", and there was a generous section of pig poetry including limericks by Roy Blount Jr. and this brilliant haiku, attributed to Frank Trippett.

> *Fall: with soulful grace*
> *the heavy-hammed swine sinks*
> *down in ooze and ahs.*

I read the book, cheered its mix of porcine fact and whimsical flight in my column, and passed it around to my colleagues. Co-workers Peggy Caldwell and Marsha Norman created their own hog-call, a piggish snort accompanied by a split-finger peace sign. Hedgepeth's pigs became stars around the newsroom, eclipsing horses until spring heralded Kentucky Derby season.

So, a few years later, when I arrived in Atlanta and was looking for potential contributors, I started trying to find Hedgepeth. I soon discovered that he was renowned in Atlanta for his command of the language, his stupendous imagination – and his inability to meet deadlines.

I introduced myself and we arranged to meet. And, not surprisingly, he had a story idea he wanted to pitch. Soon, I found myself dealing with Hedgepeth and the mystique that, I eventually realized, such encounters always create. The result was frustratingly inconclusive but still fascinating.

Atlanta, Hedgepeth told me, had a thriving subculture involving voodoo. And, underlining his argument, he had brought a small bottle of "Mystery Oil" that he had recently purchased at a drug store in Sweet Auburn, the center of Black culture just east of downtown.

The story was assigned and we agreed on a deadline, a month or so away. A week after that deadline, Hedgepeth showed up at my office. He had not finished the story, he said, but it was coming along well. "The culture is even deeper ingrained that I had been told," he said. "The details are fascinating, and I'm close to being allowed into one of the ritualistic meetings," I was assured. A new deadline was set.

A week or so after the new deadline had passed, Hedgepeth returned. This time, he said he was close, and "as collateral to my good intentions" he offered me his pocketknife, which I tried unsuccessfully to refuse.

The next time I saw him was at a reading at an Atlanta bookstore by our mutual friend, Roy Blount Jr. When I told Roy about Hedgepeth's voodoo endeavor, he chuckled. "Don't get hoo-dooed by him," he said.

I never saw the story, but the last excuse I heard from Hedgepeth tops all excuses I have heard in a half century of dealing with writers. Arriving at my office, he wanted me to return his pocketknife. "When I went to get my mail this morning," he explained, "I found a dead duck in my mailbox."

I returned his knife but kept the bottle of "Mysteria Voo Doo Oil."

Scuffling

When I decided to quit my job at *The Atlanta Journal-Constitution* in late 1993, one of my cohorts, Eileen Drennan, asked why I was leaving. After thinking about it for a moment, I said, "Because I can."

Tired of trying to please bosses for whom I had no respect and generally burnt out after almost four decades in the news business, I knew I could return to my hometown – Knoxville – and live much more cheaply than I could in Atlanta.

My dad had died a year or so earlier, aged 79, and my mother was left to manage the antique business they had established when Dad had retired from his job as a machinist at Alcoa.

Several months later I was living much as I had when I had graduated from the University of Tennessee in 1968 – in a rundown house, driving a five-year-old vehicle. But this time, the house was mine, and was mortgage-free. The small SUV was paid for, too.

Now, I figured, I could get by with occasional free-lance

writing assignments as I helped my mother and my siblings as they closed out the antiques business. And I could work on book ideas – being back in the place where I grew up, my memories would be more vivid and reflective.

My sister had become my mother's caretaker, primarily tasked with preventing her from buying more old dolls so we could liquidate her inventory of several hundred, a handful of them created in the late 1700s.

I worked at organizing my father's main contributions to the business – old farm implements and automotive memorabilia.

Uncle Jake drives the Wohlwend Bros. delivery truck

But early on, I noticed the absence of one of Dad's long-time projects. Dad grew up on Wohlwend Brothers Farm in east Knox County. My granddad and his two brothers specialized in produce, which meant that Dad was familiar with the kind of plant care that maximized profit potential. He once told me that in the 1920s, they made a seasonal fortune by growing hot-house tomatoes. "We had ripe, home-grown tomatoes a month before anyone else in Knox County," he said.

Decades later he put his gardening knowhow to use with a different kind of horticulture. He adopted a gardenia, probably acquired at a relative's post-funeral flower divvy-up. The gardenia's extravagant nature – beautiful blossoms with an intense attention-grabbing aroma – was completely opposite his own taciturn, laid-back persona.

The gardenia became his hobby long after I had left Knoxville, but I always noticed it when I visited. He saw that it was taken outside when spring had sprung, and then brought back indoors when the weather turned in early September. Even when the plant was so big that he had to use a two-wheeler to move it, he took no chances that a frost would kill it.

Thanks to my gossip-prone mother, his buddies soon were aware of the gardenia. When he would make his morning rounds in the spring, stopping at Mayford's service station or Corky's Amoco, they would rib him, asking how his gardenia was doing. His usual response was an offer to provide lapel blossoms if their wives wrangled them into wearing a suit.

When Dad died in 1993 my sister took over gardenia duty. But she was a generation away from his farm background and the gardenia only lasted through another year or so before it started to wither. When I noticed its absence from the usual cold-weather spot in the enclosed and heated porch, I asked my sister where it was. "It died in spite of everything I tried," my sister said. "I guess I didn't have Dad's touch."

Exit Polling

A year or so later, I snagged an interesting gig – polling voters as they exited precincts for a consortium of media. It was 1996, and the election involved national races. Voter News Service was at the time the premier service for exit polling; the members were the Associated Press, ABC, CBS, CNN, Fox News, and NBC.

My initial assignment involved a small precinct set up at a rural school in north Knox County, but when I scouted the location a couple of days prior to election day, I learned that the precinct had recently been combined with a larger one at Halls High School, a relatively new facility several miles away. The larger venue meant more voters, which complicated a system that was already complex.

I would set up a card table just outside the polling place and would ask exiting voters if they would fill out a questionnaire about their concerns and candidate choices. The responses would be completely anonymous.

But I would not ask each voter – my choices were dependent on the total number of registered voters at whatever precinct I was assigned. And that number would change every hour or so when I would call in my totals. One hour I might be told to ask every other voter, then the next hour it would change to every fourth voter. At one large precinct during a 1998 vote, my assignment called for approaching every 11th participant, a scrambling task.

Assignments were from the precinct's opening until its closing, and would involve a half-dozen or so call-ins from the nearest pay phone – cell phones were not yet ubiquitous. Many of the precincts were set up in public-school gymnasiums where pay phones were readily available, but, as I would learn during my final assignment, in the 2000 presidential election, sometimes the precinct could be several miles from the nearest usable telephone.

The system was designed to account for refusals and for misses, with my instructions changing every time I made my call-ins.

The 1996 assignment, involving presidential primaries as well as House and Senate races, provided an excellent introduction to the process – cooperation from often-harried precinct personnel, generally smiling and friendly reactions from voters, and in one instance, an angry invitation to step outside for further discussion.

The latter incident involved a young voter – I would guess his age at early 30s – who loudly distinguished himself when he took exception to the precinct workers' refusal to let him enter until he removed his Pat Buchanan cap. Finally, he allowed his wife to place the cap inside her purse.

A bit later, as he was exiting, he fit into my numbers game and I asked if he would participate in the exit poll. After glancing at the proffered questionnaire, he began a tirade against the "left-wing media." I told him participation was voluntary and took back my form. He wanted to keep it, so I handed it back, telling him that it was all his.

Then he wanted to know who I was voting for. By then I had to approach other exiting voters, so I ignored him. Angry now, he stepped toward me. Fortunately, his wife quickly inserted herself in front of him and pushed him toward the exit. After looking around at the attention he was drawing, he shot me a bird and let her push him outside.

Later experiences in other elections and other precincts featured encounters that were more mundane, though they presented their own problems. Twice, I was assigned to small rural precincts. One, in northeast Knox County, was distinguished in that the head of the precinct – obviously a longtime fixture – was frequently asked by voters which candidates he recommended. With side glances at my set-up, he quickly whispered his responses.

When I mailed in my paperwork the next day, I mentioned his activity, but I never heard anything about it – his flaunting of election law was not part of the Voter News Service mission.

The last election I worked – the Bush-Gore presidential race in 2000 – was also at a small rural precinct. It rained off and on and my set-up was only barely protected by an overhang. A group of the community's male voters had built a fire in a nearby metal barrel and gathered around it to smoke and catch up with the latest gossip. Their concerns – "Well, Gore wants to take away our guns and I ain't going to let that happen" – provided insights that did not surprise me. But the precinct captain's side assignment was interesting. When traffic was slow, he would stand under the overhang at my table and stop folks on their way inside to invite them to services at the nearby evangelical church he attended.

During one slow period, I made a joke about his proselytizing and whether it created a church-versus-state problem. He laughed. "I just have to make sure my wife knows that I'm making this effort – it helps keep the peace at home." Toward the end of the day, close to poll-closing time, he asked me if I thought he had invited 25 voters to his church. "At least," I answered. He grinned. "Made my quota," he said.

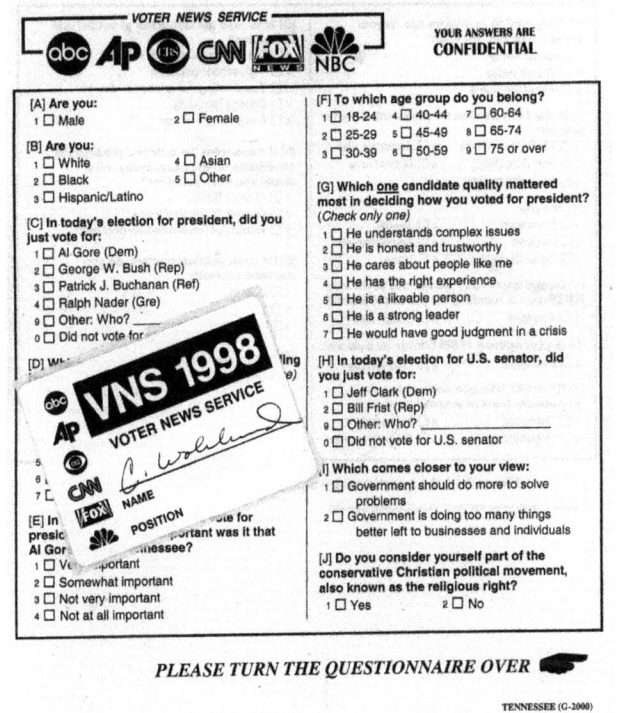

The badge I wore doing exit polls with one of the forms

Manufacturer's Rep

A part-time gig as a manufacturer's representative turned out to be another perfect scuffling job – it involved as many as 20 hours a week, making it lucrative enough to satisfy my limited needs. Plus, it was mindless and it provided entertainment. The primary locations were 17 Wal-Marts, a half-dozen K-Marts, and a couple of Targets. At the start, I was representing producers of VHS tapes, making sure the new videos were displayed properly, providing promotional buttons, sending back old releases.

Eventually I began running into another rep doing the same thing for different distributors. Cristin was full-time while I was only working a dozen or so hours a week. But she approached the job the same way I did: We both wanted to have fun while executing our duties. And we both were frequently amused – and sometimes horrified – by the actions of our fellow human beings. Soon, I was working for Cristin, sharing her more regularly scheduled duties.

The VHS business was sporadic – Hollywood's offerings weren't all blockbusters – but Cristin's duties also included making sure that the chain stores had plenty of fresh batteries available in locations conducive to impulsive purchases. Then came boxed computer software, with its games, its helpmates, its war-themed conflicts. Soon the electronic departments of our stores were featuring dozens of the boxed offerings, and we were making sure that the new versions had replaced the old and that they were properly displayed.

The software programs were guaranteed sales – what didn't sell was shipped back to the manufacturer. That meant we filled shopping carts full of the old every couple of months, took them to the Returns department and replaced them with the new versions. Frequently we would be instructed to completely reverse the order of display for the titles. And we would turn that into our own game – dodging customers as we raced down the aisles of Wal-Marts with our shopping carts loaded with boxed software, trying to make sharp turns without spilling any boxes.

Thanks to Cristin's cheerleader charm, store personnel indulged us – the department heads liked the fact that we made their jobs easier; store management liked the fact that we kept their department managers in better moods. And, as with most businesses, employee management is everything.

Cristin's effervescent smiles insured that electronics department chiefs were glad to see us and often meant that store managers would drop by to welcome us. And we quickly learned which managers were the best, and which were the slackers. And in Cristin's case, which male managers' flirtations went too far. Where those managers were a problem, I would always be with her. With one Wal-Mart location, a male store manager became such a problem that I worked that one alone,

explaining to the Problem that Cristin was busy at another site.

Another Wal-Mart employee, a female department manager, provided a different distraction when we showed up to execute a re-set early one Monday – she sported a black eye and other facial bruises. When Cristin asked about her appearance, she just shrugged and said she had gotten in a fight with her boyfriend, grinning and adding "I left him looking a lot worse than I do."

On a later visit to the same store, we watched as a shoplifter was confronted and then marched to a back office to await the police. In another theft incident, at a Knoxville store, a shoplifter walked out the front door, his loot setting off the alarm, then made his escape by boarding a city bus.

In one of the highest-volume Wal-Marts in our territory, the store manager decided to make an exception to the company's "No shoes, no shirt, no service" policy when a decidedly large customer wearing only his overalls and workboots glared at the sign and dared the female clerk to say something. After Overalls left, we shot a questioning look at the manager. "Hey, I didn't get to be boss by being stupid," he said with a laugh.

At another Knoxville Wal-Mart, we learned that members of the military were not always welcomed in stores. A store manager had confronted two uniformed soldiers. The pair – from the recruiting office – were a constant threat, the manager told us. "They're always coming in here trying to sign up our young employees," he explained.

Then there was the older gentleman who came into the electronics department, looked around, and, then asked Cristin where the records were. We then had to explain CDs to him.

At a K-Mart, the door of the locked stockroom in the back where expensive electronics were stored was always sticking, meaning the department chief had difficulty accessing items wanted by customers. One morning, as I was processing Returns, the store manager witnessed the struggle with the door, went to the hardware department, got an ax, came back and destroyed the door handle. Next time I came in the door and its frame had been replaced. I don't know how he explained the expense to his boss.

At another K-Mart I watched as a would-be customer was escorted out and told not to come back. He had been caught measuring the width of packages of baseball cards with a micrometer. It seems that avid collectors believed they had a better chance at rarities if the package had an extra card.

I retired from my rep job – by then I was working as many as 36 hours a week – when Cristin got pregnant with her second child and, facing the demands of an infant and a toddler, decided she didn't want to continue repping. Without her company, the job was no longer fun and I knew I could survive with a part-time gig teaching journalism at the University of Tennessee supplemented with occasional free-lance assignments. I only visit Wal-Mart now when I'm traveling and need to go to the bathroom – I know where they are located inside the store and I know they are generally kept clean.

The video/software work led to another mindless job – and because it involved weekend work did not interfere with other duties. I became a movie detective, responsible for making sure that theater operators were being honest with the studios that supplied them with their attractions. The following account was written for an online publication, but was never used.

Confessions of a Movie Dick

As the figures slowly sharpened into focus I realized that the suits in L.A. – always suspicious – were correct. I made a note of my findings and carefully put away the binoculars. The bosses had to be told immediately, the studio chiefs informed that their fears were justified.

I had discovered that the theater operators were not including sales tax in their ticket prices – moviegoers had to pay the listed price PLUS the added tax. And that's not the way Hollywood wanted it; they were demanding an all-inclusive price.

Yeah – the task seemed as silly as hackneyed movie-dick dialogue. But if Hollywood wanted to pay me for goofy assignments, I was willing to undertake them. The ticket-tax caper was only one gig in my career as a spy for Warner Brothers, 20th Century Fox, Sony/Columbia, Disney.

I had executed scores of house counts, tallying the number of patrons in darkened theaters. Other times I had skulked around noting the presence and positioning of film posters. Or I narked on slack-jawed teen-aged theater employees who were not wearing the proper promotional buttons. I had carefully monitored on-screen advertisements, listing their order – did Coca-Cola appear before or after Chevrolet? Audience reaction to ads was noted, too, on the rare occasions when there was any.

I had spent several years reviewing movies and had seen enough to know that the inner machinations of the film world were much more interesting than most of its products. So curiosity figured into my decision to hang out watching multiple movies at complexes on weekend nights.

Early on, I often did "blind" checks, counting the house without management being aware of my task. But soon I had switched to "open" counts, where I announced my presence upon arrival. And once I became known as an auditor, blind checks were impossible – until I figured out a way to do them while pretending that I was doing an open tally of another film.

The job involved more than just counting. The distributors wanted to know the order that the "trailers" (previews) were shown, they wanted to know what other movies were playing in the complex, they wanted to know the number of seats in each theater. There were assignments involving the attitudes of the kids working concession stands. And there were assignments that were decidedly odd.

For the movie "Independence Day," I had to note whether the sound track of the trailer was louder than the other previews. If it was not, I was to report it immediately so theater management could be set straight and the volume turned up.

Eventually, I ended up executing such assignments for two different Los Angeles-based outfits, firms that in turn contracted with 20th Century Fox, Warner Brothers, Disney, DreamWorks, Sony/Columbia. The jobs began on opening weekends, but if a movie was doing big business, second and third weekends might be added. Occasionally I would work two movies at the same theater – two films, two contractors, two distributors, two paychecks.

Though I was somewhat familiar with the ways of the industry when I drifted into house-counting, I was ignorant of the way the ticket money was divvied up. And of the tactics of the industry's marketers.

As I became friends with theater managers where I was doing open checks, I learned about the business – and one reason why Hollywood was so interested in quick information on the number of paying customers.

The distributor and the theater owner split the ticket price, with the distributor taking the biggest chunk – 90 percent or more – on opening weekend. If a movie has "legs," if it continues to draw enough crowds to warrant keeping it, by the fourth or fifth week the theater owner is taking 70 or 80 percent. One result of this kind of arrangement is that the distributors don't have much interest in a movie after the first two or three weekends. Optimally, they'll have another movie ready for a big opening. And the marketing money will be switched to the new blockbuster.

Another result is that theater owners have to make their money on concessions. Or, in the case of the complex where I did much of my checking, the theater owner reports fewer ticket sales than are actually made.

The majority of movie theaters are part of corporate chain operations, with computerized ticket sales and quick reports back to Hollywood. But there were, at least in my experience, a few independently owned theaters where the tickets were torn from an old-fashioned roll. And where there were no ticket-takers, the person selling the ticket would tear it and give the customer half. And, I soon discovered, frequently sell the other half to the next customer. The owner could then report only one ticket sale when there were actually two.

I would duly report such shenanigans and the operator would be penalized. Fox or Warner's or Disney had several ways of trying to keep the owner honest. They might refuse to give the theater a movie on the "break," – the opening weekend – offering it the third week, when most potential viewers had already seen it. Or a flawed print (this was before today's digital movies), might be provided, something that had to be noted to customers, meaning that full price could not be charged.

Ultimately, the distributor could refuse to do business with that theater.

But the most effective way was to send me in, so that the owner knew he was being watched. When doing open checks, I always made sure that the box-office worker immediately informed management that I was there.

The most difficult assignments were blind checks, when I would spend all day in the complex, counting the customers at each showing of the assigned movie. I would purchase tickets only for the first matinee and the first evening shows, then count as many as five additional screenings without paying.

I experimented with disguises – switching baseball caps, removing my glasses, going to my car and changing jackets. But finally I realized that the kids tearing the tickets could care less if they saw the same person coming and going all day long.

Once, for a "Spiderman" opening, the feature was playing on three different screens, 15 minutes apart. All were close to sell-outs, which meant 250 or so customers in each theater. I had to count number 1 in a hurry, then slip into theater number 2, tally again, go to number 3 and count again. No one ever questioned me.

Sometimes the assignments were puzzling. Once, I drew graph-paper maps of theater layouts, noting the location of the box office, the concession stand and their relation to the screens the film I was checking was playing on. Was the distributor worried that the popcorn was too far away from the moviegoers?

Of course I was free to watch movies without paying and sometimes did. But most films I had no interest in viewing. I counted the house 16 straight weekends for the blockbuster "Titanic" – and never watched more than the first 15 or 20 minutes of it. Conversely, I saw "Get Shorty" six times in one weekend, and loved it every time. Sometimes the starting times and number of screens meant I could not watch a movie from start to finish. I saw bits and pieces of "Ray" over three days, finally figuring that I had seen it all at least once.

Sometimes I would go into a nearly empty theater, preferably one that was showing a movie that did not feature a lot of explosions, and sleep. Often, I sat in the lobby and read a book I brought along.

Once, I was sitting in the lobby when a teen-ager sat down next to me. He wanted to know what I was reading. I showed him. Then he asked if I was reading it for "a class or something." When I told him no, that I was reading it because I wanted to, he was flabbergasted. Reading for pleasure, it seems, was a concept unknown to him.

But I should not have been surprised, given the clientele of that particular complex. The kids cleaning up frequently found empty liquor bottles; cigarette-lighter burns were evident all over the wall-carpeting; Gummy bears periodically had to be removed from screens where they had been thrown; and off-screen fights sometimes occurred.

Management was involved in one such encounter. A religious patron stormed out of a theater complaining about the sexual content of one of the trailers. When the patron angrily kicked the door of the box office, the manager started after him before being restrained by a couple of his employees. I watched from a distance, relishing the sight of religious-based violence over make-believe movie sex.

Sometimes I counted interesting films – movies I would have reviewed favorably – that were quickly left to die by the distributor. "Bulworth," "Home Fries" and "The Fighting Temptations" come to mind.

I discovered after a while that sometimes when I was checking on theater management, the movie distributor was checking on me. For example, while I would be working an open check, another checker might be counting the same movie blind. If I noticed someone watching the first 15 minutes of the same movie for the third time, from a seat in the rear, then I knew that person was probably an auditor, working a blind for a different contractor. Hollywood, true to its traditions, trusts no one. And no one is more aware of that than theater owners.

I heard from longtime managers about the strongarm tactics of distributors, about being forced to take two or even three prints of a particular movie at it's opening, of being cajoled into continuing to screen a feature in the room with the most seats, whether the numbers justified it or not. And I found general consensus on the most-demanding and difficult distributor:

Disney. None of the theater managers had anything good to say about Mickey's minions.

Despite the opportunities to view the blockbuster-of-the-moment for free, I found most of my movie entertainment came from the management and employees of the theaters.

If management was cheating the distributor, the smarter kids quickly figured out what was happening. And figured that if the owner could cheat, they could, too. When the coast was clear, they did not hesitate to allow their friends in for free. I just made sure they knew not to allow them into whatever film I was counting.

At one of my last blind-check assignments, I surprised a teen-age usher opening a back door to allow four of his friends to slip in. I was on my way into "Oceans 11" to watch it for the third or fourth time (it was in its 11th week) between counts of another film. As George Clooney and company set up their complex con, I decided not to report the usher. After all, I, too, was running a con, hiding in the dark, beating the theater owner out of $10.

Wordplay

At some point in the early days of Twitter, a conversation with fellow East Tennessee native James Noel Smith led me to begin playing around with haiku – Tweets, with their character limitations, were the perfect venue. Eventually, I created about three dozen Hillbilly Haiku, many inspired by James Noel's observations. Included here is a sampling, with illustrations by James Noel, Jan Bryza, and Melissa Wozniak.

The haiku led to experiments with more complicated poetic forms – sonnets, blues and a villanelle.

The haiku begin with memories of childhood incidents, a couple reference my time living in Texas, and the remainder are more general in subject matter. Three were illustrated by James Noel Smith (marked JNS), two by Melissa Wozniak (MW), and one by Jan Bryza (JB).

Who peed in your pants,
teacher asked when I was five.
Roy Rogers, I said.

~~~

Housing a green snake
inside my locker – till he
left home, trailing screams.

~~~

Seventh-grade classmate
taken by cops one day, an
unwilling dropout.

~~~

Shop initiative:
converting a cap pistol
to a crude zip gun.

In school parking lot
ninth grader's Merc gets rubber –
and our attention.

Teacher is snoring
in civics class, so we learn
about Anarchy.

LaFong speeds beauty
across Texas, disdainful
of any waltzing.

Back-row marbles drop;
study-hall teacher chases a
multitude of pings.

Loud math-class squawking
as a live rooster escapes
teacher's desk drawer.

MW

~~~

Turn of tap puts end
to a shower-room card game,
losers doubly soaked.

~~~

Smug laughter stifled
as proud pair of old ladies
show off new tattoos.

~~~

Eenie's Eats, Teek's Bar,
Henderlight's, or Vernon's Bait,
the cap has to fit.

No girls to astound,
Rollo joins the bar skeptics
with a new hustle.

New technology leads
to burst of old-school cursing
on printshop deadline.

A hand knit tailwarmer
is a must for the cool cats
on their nightly rounds.

At Lunch

When I was 14 in Albuquerque,
a car hop so Latino, so exotic,
I stared, stuck to seat and silent,
as she added a radiant smile
to a pair of tacos loaded with pollo,
her cheery look the special sauce.
Then in Maine decades later, crabcakes
delivered by a blonde beauty spending
her summer earning beach money
indulging me, the baldly obvious flirt,
a good-natured reminder of the car hop
of my teens, sleek Southwestern grace
the other side of the country,
the other side of innocence.

WESTWARD 1981

Magazine office full of arrogance,
an adult playpen aswirl with male ego,
writers romp in a nimble word dance.
Heated exchanges about picture play
as photographers line up images:
"These are the must-haves," they say.
Newsroom escapees sneer with scorn,
as haughty editor turns a headline phrase
while others tout opinions of jealousy born.
The wizened vet, stained by printer's ink,
drains his umpteenth coffee and welcomes
the female newcomer, flashing a sly wink
as noisy arguments continue to unfurl,
her smile adding grace to an unruly world.

Reflection

Intimacies past but not forgotten:
Just a couple of miles east of the Glades,
a nightly escape, pooling and cooling;
vivid flashes from Louisville and Dallas;
or Kansas City, ice-bound in winter.
Atlanta maybe? Knoxville early or late?
Images crystal clear, eyes that always smile,
some dark, mysterious; others blue and bright.
One special look dashes past, a shade of slate.
Grins often break out, most sweet and shy,
others dissolving into familiar laughter
before ending with a glance that's oh so sly.
But the wheres and whens matter not
for memories as fresh as these bon mots.

Jukebox, 1969

A villanelle about a co-ed named June
at the start of fall semester in September.

June in September,
listening to the records,
and baby it's you.

Flirting on the stoop
bare thighs pressing,
June in September.

Laughing with the tune
Little Latin Lupe Lu,
still, baby it's you.

You want to take a ride
though we've no Detroit wheels,
June in September.

Halter top and short shorts,
neither devil nor dress of blue,
still, baby it's you.

Three years later,
a starched world away.
Still, baby it's you,
June in September.

~~~

Early one afternoon as I was leaving the UT Aquatic Center, I noticed a trio of motorcycles parked next to the indoor-pool building. The harsh light left the bikes in striking contrast. The motorcycles resembled giant insects. The academic setting inspired a pseudo-scientific explanation:

A family of Common Kawasaki Ninjas

Unrealized Concepts

My first afternoon-newspaper employer was *The Louisville Times*, sister publication of *The Courier-Journal*. The two papers, owned by the Bingham family when I was employed there from 1975 until 1980, shared newsroom space. That meant that deadlines were strictly followed – desks and other facilities had to be vacated by *Times* personnel at about 3 p.m. to be taken over by C-J employees arriving for their nighttime shifts.

Those of us finishing up mid-afternoon were frequently still wired from deadline chaos. And that meant calm-down time at a nearby hangout. Teek's announced its presence with the motto "World-Famous New York Bar" on the sign overhanging the front door.

And the claim may have been legitimate. When one of the owners was charged with making book (we're talking about a bar in a horse-racing town), the feds in charge of the case worked out a plea deal that ensured that his absence would not affect Teek's. He was allowed to serve his sentence on weekends so the prosecution could still enjoy their Teek's time. Such an arrangement could have made it famous, at least among federal law-enforcement personnel.

On any given afternoon Teek's would be busy with journalists talking about stories, complaining about decisions from on high, or trying to ferret information from the lawyers who had ducked in from the federal offices a block away.

One example of a story born at Teek's: Complaints about the offerings on the jukebox one afternoon led to an all-over-town survey and resulting story touting Louisville's "best" jukeboxes as determined by their featured music. It was a fun assignment that garnered letters-to-the-editor for several weeks – the dancers who liked big-band music arguing with those who preferred beach tunes.

But often the talk would grow around absurd ideas tossed out just for laughs. Often, the offering had its origin in an idiotic idea proposed by a section chief.

An example we thought idiotic that was assigned: An editor, frustrated by telephone calls leaving her on hold with canned music, wanted a story about that irritating practice. A dozen calls later and the reporter had to tell her that none of the people she talked to objected to the music. Eventually, after another dozen attempts, the editor let the idea die.

When I moved to Dallas in 1980 to work on the *Times Herald's* Sunday magazine, I faced a new set of bosses, but I soon realized that the mind-set was not that different from what I had dealt with in Louisville. Dallas was the site of a newspaper war – the traditionally afternoon *Times Herald* had recently been purchased by Times-Mirror whose flagship was *The Los Angeles Times*. The new owners immediately changed publication times to all-day, which meant that we were now engaged in a head-to-head battle with *The Dallas Morning News*, locally owned.

Because I was working on a weekly publication, my schedule was more normal than it had been in Louisville – 9 to 5, except for Fridays, which always went to about 7 p.m. when our assembled pages had to be shipped to our roto-gravure printer, which was part of the Bingham empire in Louisville.

But unwind time was still necessary. There were several joints of choice in Dallas, ranging from funkiness (Louie's) to sleek hipness (the 8.0). And idiotic story ideas from competing section-editor bosses still were part of the conversation.

This part of "Remnants & Reflections" – Unrealized Concepts – is concerned with some of those proposals, most that were tossed around as jokes, but others that we tried to bring to fruition. Though we thought our ideas were clever we failed to convince anyone else.

Cat Tales

The first is a collaboration that was born shortly after I became the caretaker of a kitten. James Noel Smith's girlfriend, Michelle, had rescued a very young, solid-black kitten. "His mother abandoned him," she said. "And he's too young to fend for himself. Give him warm milk for a week or so then switch him to real food." So, despite my protests, I now had a feline boarder. I named him Spot.

After I left for work the next day, he found what became a favorite hiding place – the bottom drawer of my desk, which I had accidentally left cracked open. He had managed to get in, but his meows on my arrival indicated that he could not get out.

He quickly got over his initial fears and soon had the run of my apartment. Still a kitten, he survived my move to Kansas City a month or so later, and soon charmed my new landlady, who would stand outside my door when I was at work and talk to him.

One day I came home from work and opened the door to a toilet-paper trail. Spot had managed to pull it from its bathroom container, then down the hall, across the living room and then to the foyer – without breaking it.

That accomplishment led to an idea for a whimsical book: Exploring the activities of cats while their keepers are away.

I talked the idea over with another talented Dallas friend, illustrator/designer Jan Bryza. Also a cat owner, she quickly signed on to supply the drawings. We produced several examples.

Though cats were having a moment in the early 1980s, we could not interest a publisher and the idea died. Of course, once the Internet came along, accompanied by smart phones capable of video, cat owners started capturing their pets pulling all kinds of stunts and posting them on YouTube, proving that the fanciful tales Jan and I produced were not quite as absurd as they seemed. Our samples follow.

～～～

Roger Thomas, a plumber from Oakbrook, Illinois, made

an interesting discovery on a house call from a man who reported "something" was stopping up his bathtub drain.

"The customer had to go to work so he left the key under the mat. I got there about 11 in the morning, let myself in and went into the bathroom. There, in the tub, surrounded by bubbles, was this cat, a big yellow, short-hair. He was laying back, had a big cigar in his mouth, and was reading the newspaper. When he saw me, you can bet he jumped out of that tub real quick. Of course cat hair was the problem. I told the owner about what I had seen, but he didn't believe me. I never told nobody else."

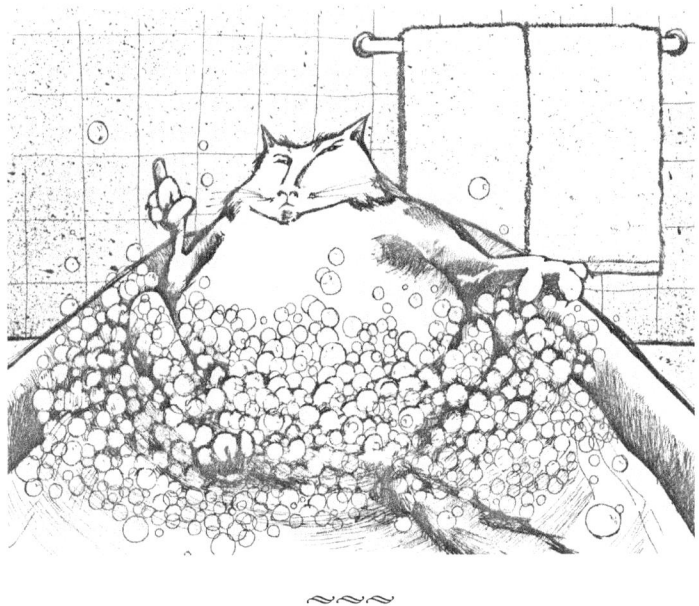

Ida V., a 29-year-old who is in sales in Richmond, Virginia, returned home late one Sunday after a seminar to find her 2-year-old white Persian female, Tabatha, acting in an unusual manner.

"I had been gone for three days and my neighbor had been looking in on Tabs. But when I opened the door, instead of running in to see me like she always does, Tabs ran away and hid under the couch. At first I thought my neighbor had done something to her. (She can be weird, you know, especially when she's in her Elvira mode.) When I finally coaxed Tabs out with some treats, I saw that she had a bright stripe of something pink down her back and had a safety pin in her ear. I didn't know what to think, and Tabs was no help. She just acted like nothing was wrong. Naturally, Tabs ran off the first chance she got. My weird neighbor insists that she later saw her skulking around some punk-music dive over in Virginia Beach."

Miss V. now owns a dog.

~·~·~

Jim Kindall, a free-lance social critic from Kansas City, returned home to retrieve a forgotten ham sandwich one morning and discovered that his furniture had been rearranged by his two cats, Hap (not her real name) and Blackie.

"It was amazing. I don't know how they did it. The sofa had been moved a good 10 feet; a Naugahyde recliner was where the sofa had been and a bookcase had been pushed to the opposite wall. Judging by her appearance, the whole thing was Hap's idea. She was lying on the sofa, looking fat and sassy, while Blackie paced back and forth. You can bet they both ran when I came in. I didn't have time to move the furniture back,

and went on to work. When I came home that evening the furniture was back where it belonged, and Blackie was lying on the couch while Hap sulked. I wrote a paper about it but none of the journals was interested. Says something about the male-female relationship, I guess."

Longhorn Ballroom

A *Times Herald* going-away party was the scene of another story idea that almost came to be. *Westward's* art director, Fred Woodward, was moving to Austin to take over the design duties of *Texas Monthly*. The party site was a longtime Dallas fixture, the Longhorn Ballroom.

Besides Fred, the participants included a diverse group. Amy Cunningham and Iris Krasnow both had spent parts of their childhoods in Chicago, Steve Reddicliffe came to Dallas from Miami, Ande Zellman is a Boston native. James Noel Smith, like me, is from East Tennessee, and a couple of others are Texans, familiar with what was expected on the Longhorn's dancefloor. They warned us that we should be respectful of Texas tradition, but we ignored them.

One of our party, Matt Drace, introduced his version of The Pogo to the dance floor and he, Fred and Iris quickly Pogoed their way to dance-floor stardom. Then as the band ended their set, Iris did an expert Split. It was, her neighboring dancer said, "the first time I've ever seen anybody do that here and I've been a regular for 25 years."

Back at our table, it was decided that Amy should do a story proposing an effort to modernize the Longhorn's dance-floor doings. Fred of course had several ideas for the design and illustration. Fortunately, the idea was soon forgotten. And as far as we know, Iris's stunt has never been duplicated.

~~~

Buffalo George

Not long after I arrived in Dallas I had been introduced to another Dallas tradition – freelancer George Toomer, a popular fixture of the city's creative circle. Physically, Toomer looked the part of an Old West legend. He was about 6 foot 2, weighed around 250 pounds and sported a full beard. Add a booming voice to his off-the-wall creative mind and a healthy skepticism toward the power-structure version of

the city, and you have an in-demand force. Literally powering this force, George's vehicle of choice was a classic car – a 1951 Hudson Hornet that he called Blaze the Wonder Horse.

One of Toomer's working partners was a broadcast specialist who had worked in the Baltimore area. The pair began a successful project that featured Toomer as a deadpan on-air reviewer of fast-food offerings. Once a month, he would fly to Baltimore and be driven around the city in a limo to sample drive-through fare, his filmed comments were then edited to a short segment that aired as a weekly television-news spot.

The show was successful enough that the pair started looking for something similar for Dallas. They hit upon the idea of a 15-minute intro for a late-night movie. Toomer would host a couple of talent acts then segue into introducing the movie.

For the talent, he would draw on his friends and then add other acts as the show built its audience. Toomer invited me to the show's first audition, set for a Sunday afternoon at the Esquire Theater, an old movie venue that was now available for rent. James Noel Smith agreed to join the festivities as moral support.

Already lined up were a couple of Toomer's like-minded friends, – a Fort Worth cowboy who did rope tricks, and another pal who specialized in working with a Yo-Yo. When Toomer urged me to participate, I came up with an idea involving my singing an old vaudeville ditty I had learned decades earlier while working at Boy Scout camp. The subject was watermelon rinds and the chorus involved schlurping sounds. I would introduce the song with a serious intro about how much the song meant to me, delivered deadpan.

A handful of others had responded to an ad announcing the auditions, the most promising being a dentist who played the musical saw. The producer warmed up the 30 or 40 fun-seekers in the audience with the rope trickster and the Yo-Yo artist, Toomer keeping things moving with his jokes and comments.

Then the dentist – obviously serious about his talent – volunteered to go on next. After an accomplished rendition of "Turkey in the Straw", he was asked what other tunes he could do. "I can play anything," he said.

"What about "Yellow Rose of Texas?" Toomer asked. So that was next. The dentist, proud of himself and unaware that maybe the show was not meant to be serious was asked if he could play "Take Five," the Dave Brubeck jazz standard in 5/4 time. He asked if someone would hum it for him – the up-the-sleeves response made him realize that he was not being taken seriously – that the idea of the entire show was meant as comedy. He packed up his saw and left.

After an accordion solo and a vocal duo, the producer announced that our time in the theater was at an end. So I never got to sing the watermelon song. And George and his pals moved on to other projects, memories of the sawing dentist relegated to a running joke, the story shared when we were bored.

And, finally...

The last item in this section is from James Noel Smith. In the early 2000s, after both of us had moved back to East Tennessee, we noticed the pop-culture phenomenon of the moment – the popularity of adding "extreme" as part of the description of an activity. So we end Unrealized Concepts involved in "extreme waiting."

Acknowledgements

I owe much of this project's completion to my work colleagues from decades in the news business. Most are named in the relevant accounts.

The Wandering section begins with accounts of 1972 and 1973 trips to Europe, which were made richer by the staff of United Press International in Brussels, who were generous in sharing knowledge and advice. And the three weeks I spent traversing the Soviet Union in 1977 would not have been successful without the knowledge and guidance of Lilya Lochanko.

My fellow travelers for the At Speed section were Steve Horne and the late Tom Stokes. Fortunately, we took dozens of photographs that helped free up memories.

Talented writers, illustrators and photographers who shared my interests and outlook provided encouragement. In alphabetical order, thanks to John Anderson, Jim Bennett, Jan Bryza, Amy Cunningham, Charlie Daniel, Bruce Hight, Larry Hobbs, Jim Kindall, Michael Larkin, Edgar Miller, Sean Mitchell, Tom Owens, James Noel Smith, Vince Staten, Susan Stewart, Fred Woodward, and Melissa Wozniak.

Cousin Judy Wohlwend graciously provided proof-reading assistance.

Finally, the book's existence was made possible through the efforts of designer and tech expert Bill Davison, who calmly indulged my frequent additions, corrections, and subtractions.

www.ingramcontent.com/pod-product-compliance
Lightning Source LLC
Chambersburg PA
CBHW061744070526
44585CB00025B/2801